THE BEATITUDES

THE BEATITUDES

LIVING IN SYNC WITH THE REIGN OF GOD

Darrell W. Johnson

Regent College Publishing
www.regentpublishing.com

Published 2015 by Regent College Publishing

Regent College Publishing
5800 University Boulevard, Vancouver, BC V6T 2E4 Canada
Web: www.regentpublishing.com
E-mail: info@regentpublishing.com

Regent College Publishing is an imprint of the Regent Bookstore <www.regentbookstore.com>. Views expressed in works published by Regent College Publishing are those of the author and do not necessarily represent the official position of Regent College <www.regent-college.edu>.

ISBN 978-1-57383-522-0

Cataloguing in Publication information is on file at Library and Archives Canada.

All Scripture quotations, unless otherwise indicated, are taken from the New American Standard Bible, copyright 1995 by the Lockman Foundation.

To Mary and Paul,
who have embodied the Beatitudes for me
ever since I married your daughter.

TABLE OF CONTENTS

INTRODUCTION
THE EMERGING OF A
NEW HUMANITY

"On first reading [the Sermon on the Mount] you feel that it
turns everything upside down, but the second time you
read it you discover that it turns everything right
side up. The first time you read it you feel that
it is impossible; the second time, you feel
that nothing else is possible." [1]

They were sitting in a kind of natural amphitheater, on a sloping hill beside the Sea of Galilee. Some were rough fishermen with their hired hands. Some were shrewd tax-collectors and their cronies. Uptight religious leaders, like the Pharisees and the Sadducees, were there because they were growing increasingly curious and nervous about the new Preacher in Palestine. There were hard-working tradespeople of all sorts, as well as mothers with their children. They were all, really, ordinary people—broken, hurting, and scared. They were people like me... and like you.

Something was happening in their towns and villages. And it was happening because of the new Preacher who had arrived on the scene with what He called "the gospel of God." He had been joyfully announcing, everywhere He traveled,

---

1 G.K. Chesterton as quoted in E. Stanley Jones, *The Christ of the Mount: A Working Philosophy of Life* (Nashville: Abingdon, 1931), 14.

the good news that history had reached a major turning point. "The time is fulfilled," He said, "the kingdom of God has come near." So near—because of Him, and in Him.

And things had started happening! People were being cured of diseases. Those who had long suffered blindness were beginning to see. The lame were beginning to walk. People long held captive by demonic spirits were being set free. People were experiencing the joy of having their sins forgiven. Troubled minds were finding peace.

So from all over Galilee, people were flocking to the Preacher, to Jesus of Nazareth. I would have, and I think you would have too.

LIFE-CHANGING WORDS

On that hillside, standing before a diverse assembly of human beings, Jesus spoke some of the most revolutionary words ever spoken. Jesus spoke "the Beatitudes," as they have come to be called. Eight "Blessed are…" statements, through which Jesus began to describe the kind of people who begin to emerge when the kingdom of God starts to break into the world.

Matthew the tax-collector, who later became a follower of the Preacher, was there that day, and he wrote down Jesus' words in the first twelve verses of the fifth chapter of the book that bears his name, the New Testament document we call "The Gospel according to Matthew."

Throughout the centuries since they were written down, Jesus' words have leapt off the page and are found all over the place in our world—on posters and greeting cards, hanging on walls, emailed out by people who have no idea who spoke them. The fact is, these words ought to come with a cautionary label: "Warning! Let these words loose and your world will get rocked!"

In this book, I invite you to join me—so to speak—in that natural amphitheater, and give Jesus a fresh hearing. I invite you to join me at His feet, and for the first time or for the hundredth time, to listen to words which, when embraced, bring about the emerging of a new kind of humanity.

Listen:

When Jesus saw the crowds, He went up on the mountain; and after He sat down, His disciples came to Him. He opened His mouth and began to teach them, saying,

> *"Blessed are the poor in spirit,*
> *for theirs is the kingdom of heaven.*
> *Blessed are those who mourn,*
> *for they shall be comforted.*
> *Blessed are the gentle,*
> *for they shall inherit the earth.*
> *Blessed are those who hunger and thirst*
> *for righteousness,*
> *for they shall be satisfied.*
> *Blessed are the merciful,*
> *for they shall receive mercy.*
> *Blessed are the pure in heart,*
> *for they shall see God.*
> *Blessed are the peacemakers,*
> *for they shall be called sons of God.*
> *Blessed are those who have been persecuted*
> *for the sake of righteousness,*
> *for theirs is the kingdom of heaven.*

*Blessed are you when people insult you and persecute you,
and falsely say all kinds of evil against you because of Me.
Rejoice and be glad, for your reward in heaven is great;
for in the same way they persecuted the prophets who were
before you.*

(Matthew 5:1-12)

THE CONTEXT OF THESE LIFE-CHANGING WORDS

Now, as is the case with all sayings of all the great preachers and sages of history, Jesus' Beatitudes need to be heard and seen in the context in which He first spoke them. As E. Stanley Jones, the Methodist missionary to India (whom I will quote often in this book) helped me see, if we separate His Beatitudes from the context in which He first spoke them, His words, meant to give life, become either frustrating idealism or oppressive legalism.[2]

So, let us begin by spending some time in the context:

*Now when Jesus heard that John had been taken into custody,
He withdrew into Galilee; and leaving Nazareth, He came
and settled in Capernaum, which is by the sea, in the region
of Zebulun and Naphtali. This was to fulfill what was spoken
through Isaiah the prophet:*

> *"The land of Zebulun and the land of Naphtali,
> By the way of the sea, beyond the Jordan, Galilee of
> the Gentiles—
> The people who were sitting in darkness saw a
> great Light,
> And those who were sitting in the land and shadow of death,
> Upon them a Light dawned."*

---

2 Ibid., 31-34.

From that time Jesus began to preach and say, "Repent, for the kingdom of heaven is at hand."

Now as Jesus was walking by the Sea of Galilee, He saw two brothers, Simon who was called Peter, and Andrew his brother, casting a net into the sea; for they were fishermen. And He said to them, "Follow Me, and I will make you fishers of men." Immediately they left their nets and followed Him. Going on from there He saw two other brothers, James the son of Zebedee, and John his brother, in the boat with Zebedee their father, mending their nets; and He called them. Immediately they left the boat and their father, and followed Him.

Jesus was going throughout all Galilee, teaching in their synagogues and proclaiming the gospel of the kingdom, and healing every kind of disease and every kind of sickness among the people.

The news about Him spread throughout all Syria; and they brought to Him all who were ill, those suffering with various diseases and pains, demoniacs, epileptics, paralytics; and He healed them. Large crowds followed Him from Galilee and the Decapolis and Jerusalem and Judea and from beyond the Jordan.

(Matthew 4:12-25)

Matthew is careful to help us realize that Jesus first spoke His Beatitudes, and the rest of His Sermon on the Mount, right after He first announced His gospel, His good news. He speaks His Beatitudes in the context of gospel. This is crucial to grasp and remember.

So we need to ask, "What is Jesus' good news?" This is the second most important question we can ever ask, the most important being, "Who is Jesus?"[3] Who is this Jesus, who walks into our lives and calls us to follow Him into a whole new kind of life? Who is this Jesus, who promises a different quality of life to everyone who will journey with Him? And then, the second question follows: What is the good news He brings? Jesus is, after all, the first good-news-izer, the first evangelist, the first bringer of the gospel. So we ask, "What is His good news for the world?"

Jesus puts it in one line, one massively transformative line: "Repent, for the kingdom of heaven is at hand" (Matthew 4:17). The gospel according to Jesus of Nazareth is the explosive announcement that in Him and because of Him, the long-awaited kingdom of the Living God is breaking into the world! In and because of Jesus, the long-awaited reign of heaven is breaking in upon the earth!

In the Gospel according to Mark, we have an expanded version of Jesus' announcement of His gospel. Mark 1:15 gives us the only definition of the gospel that Jesus ever gave. Mark tells us that after John the Baptist had been put in prison, Jesus came into Galilee "preaching the gospel of God." And this is what Jesus said: "The time is fulfilled, and the kingdom of God is at hand. Repent and believe in the gospel."

Do you hear the radical news Jesus is announcing? The gospel according to Jesus is the announcement of a great fact that impacts all other facts. The gospel according to Jesus is

---

3 For more on this question, see my book *Who is Jesus?* (Vancouver: Regent College Publishing, 2011).

that in Him, and because of Him, history has reached a major crisis point—"The time is fulfilled." We are now passing from one era into a whole new era. The gospel according to Jesus is that in Him, and because of Him, the long-awaited, glorious, re-creating reign of God is invading the world.

The gospel according to Jesus is good news not only because our sins have been forgiven and we are acquitted before the Judge of the universe. The gospel according to Jesus is good news not only because we are adopted into the family of God. The gospel according to Jesus is good news not only because we have been given the gift of eternal life. The gospel according to Jesus is such good news because God's new world order is breaking into our brokenness. The gospel according to Jesus is such good news because, as David Wenham of England puts it, "The longed-for [divine] revolution is now under way."[4] "The people who walk in darkness will see a great light; those who live in a dark land, the light will shine on them" (Isaiah 9:2). The future is breaking into the present; heaven is invading earth.

Understandably, Jesus couples His announcement of this great fact with a call to change our thinking. "Repent, for the kingdom of heaven is at hand" (Matthew 4:17). "Repent and believe in the gospel [the good news]" (Mark 1:15). "Repent" simply means "think again" or "think anew." More simply, it means "turn around." "You have been heading in the wrong direction. Make a U-turn and believe My good news." "The time is fulfilled; the kingdom of God has come near; make a

---

4 David Wenham, *The Parables of Jesus* (Downers Grove: InterVarsity Press, 1989), 22.

U-turn in the road, embrace Me and My gospel, and put your weight on My good news."

It is in that context that Jesus speaks His Beatitudes.

And here is the implication for our understanding of His words: The clearest sign that human beings are in fact "turning around and believing" is that they are becoming "Beatitude people." The clearest sign that human beings are in fact making a U-turn and embracing Jesus and His gospel is that they are becoming "blessed-are people."

Another way to make the point: In His Beatitudes, Jesus is painting a portrait of people in whom He and His gospel are taking hold. Jesus is giving a profile of people who are making a U-turn and welcoming Him and His kingdom. He is drawing a sketch of those in whom God's new world order is emerging, those upon whom the light of grace is dawning. In His Beatitudes, Jesus is painting a portrait of those who, in the language of the Gospel of John, are being "born again from above" (John 3:3, my translation). In His Beatitudes, Jesus has put together a profile of kingdom-people, twice-born people, Spirit-filled people. Jesus is describing a humanity transformed by Him and His good news.

THE COMING OF THE KINGDOM

Maybe a diagram would help at this point. The diagram puts Jesus and His gospel into historical context.

The diagram is a time line of the Living God's dealing with humanity.[5]

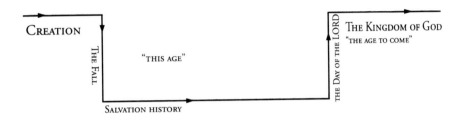

The time line begins with creation and leads to the new creation. It begins with God creating the heaven and the earth and humanity within it, and leads to God re-creating the heaven and the earth and humanity within it.

We begin with God speaking us into being in His good world. We then move to the sad and tragic decision humans made to "go it alone"—to no longer trust God to be God, and to take our lives into our own hands. We fell.

It was then that we first encountered the God of mercy and grace. For no sooner had we rebelled against God than He made a promise to one day come and undo the ruin we caused. In the now-fallen world, in the garden that was becoming a cemetery, God began what is called "salvation history." And as God unfolded His plan, it became clear that history was being moved toward a day, a great day, "the Day of the LORD," as the prophets of the Old Testament called it.

---

5 I've adapted the diagram from one that I received from Professor George Ladd, the Biblical scholar to whom I owe the greatest debt. For more information, see George Eldon Ladd, *A Theology of the New Testament*, ed. Donald A. Hagner, rev. ed. (Grand Rapids: William B. Eerdmans, 1993), 66-67.

1. On that day, God would radically intervene in history and bring His plan to fulfillment.

2. On that day, sin would be removed, evil would be overcome and banished, and death would be no more.

3. On that day, the kingdom of God would come into the world.

Now, here is the gospel according to Jesus of Nazareth:

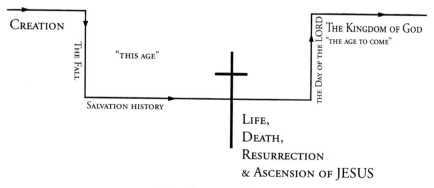

"THE KINGDOM OF GOD HAS COME NEAR."

Ahead of the great day, God comes into the world. As Matthew tells us in the Christmas story (a few chapters before the Beatitudes), Jesus is Immanuel, God with us, or more literally, the with-us-God. Ahead of the great day of the LORD, the Lord Himself comes into the world and brings with Him His kingdom.

The cross on the diagram stands for all that is involved in Jesus' coming: His birth, His life, His ministry, His death, His resurrection, His ascension, and His pouring out of the Holy Spirit. The coming of Jesus, the with-us-God, is the coming of the kingdom of God. In Jesus' coming near, the kingdom of God has come near ahead of time—ahead of the great day of the LORD!

Jesus' gospel is the announcement of this great fact: the future is spilling over into the present, and heaven is invading the earth.

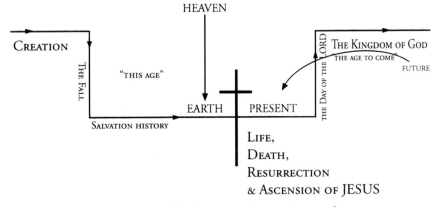

"The Kingdom of God has come near."

It is in this context that Jesus first speaks His Beatitudes. Separate Jesus' Beatitudes from Jesus' gospel, and they become either frustrating idealism or oppressive legalism.

In His Beatitudes, Jesus is simply describing what happens to human beings when His gospel grabs hold. In His Beatitudes, Jesus is giving a profile of the new humanity that happens, the new humanity that emerges, when the reign of God breaks into our brokenness. Jesus is describing people in sync with that great fact.

1

PRELIMINARY OBSERVATIONS

MATTHEW 5:3-12

Before we begin to make our way through Jesus' Beatitudes one at a time, I want to make a number of observations about the Beatitudes as a whole.

THE PACKAGING OF THE BEATITUDES

First, notice how the eight Beatitudes are packaged. Jesus brackets them with the phrase, "theirs is the kingdom." The first and eighth statements have the same reason for blessedness—"theirs is the kingdom." Beatitude one: "Blessed are the poor in spirit, for theirs is the kingdom." (Note also that He does not say, "theirs will be the kingdom," but "theirs is the kingdom.") Beatitude eight: "Blessed are those who are persecuted for righteousness' sake, for theirs is the kingdom of heaven." (And again, it is not "theirs will be the kingdom," but "theirs is the kingdom.")

Now, because all eight are bracketed by "theirs is the kingdom," I think it is exegetically sound to read that phrase after each Beatitude. Blessed are the poor in spirit, for theirs is the kingdom of heaven. But also,

> Blessed are those who mourn, for theirs is the kingdom.
> Blessed are the meek, for theirs is the kingdom.
> Blessed are those who hunger and thirst for righteousness,
>   for theirs is the kingdom.
> Blessed are the merciful, for theirs is the kingdom.
> Blessed are the pure in heart, for theirs is the kingdom.
> Blessed are the peacemakers, for theirs is the kingdom.

This means that the specific blessings promised in the second through seventh Beatitudes are different dimensions of the in-breaking kingdom of God—different ways of saying what this means. Looking at how the whole is packaged, we discover what God's new order is all about! It is about being comforted (5:4). It is about inheriting the earth (5:5; note that this keeps us from over-spiritualizing the kingdom). It is about receiving our desire for righteousness, for right-relatedness, for justice (5:6). It is about receiving mercy (5:7). It is about seeing God (5:8; the greatest blessing of all)! It is about being called and treated as children of God (5:9). The whole package is wrapped in "theirs is the kingdom."

THE EMPHATIC THEIR/THEY

Notice also the position of the pronoun (their/they). "Theirs" literally is "of them." In the original, the pronoun stands at the beginning of the clause for emphasis. It is not "for the kingdom is theirs," but "theirs is the kingdom." It is not "see God they shall," but "they shall see God." The implication is "theirs and only theirs," "them and only them," and "they and only they." When we read the Beatitudes with this emphasis, we hear just how radical they are.

> Blessed are the poor in spirit,
>> for theirs, and only theirs,
>> is the kingdom of heaven.
> Blessed are the meek,
>> for they, and only they,
>> shall inherit the earth.
> Blessed are the pure in heart,
>> for they, and only they,
>> shall see God.
> Blessed are the peacemakers,
>> for they, and only they,
>> shall be called the children of God.
> Blessed are those who are persecuted for righteousness' sake,
>> for theirs, and only theirs,
>> is the kingdom.

To make the point more boldly, Jesus is saying that those who are not poor in spirit have not yet received the kingdom. Those who are not meek will not inherit the earth. Those who are not peacemakers are not acting as children of God. Those who are not persecuted are not yet living the kingdom life.

THE UNITY OF THE BEATITUDES

Another observation: Jesus is not describing eight differ-ent persons, but is describing eight different qualities of the same person.[1] Jesus is not describing eight different kinds of kingdom people; rather, He is describing eight interrelated qualities that emerge in every "kingdomized" person. Jesus is not saying that when His gospel grabs hold, one of us becomes poor in spirit, another of us becomes meek, and another gets hungry and thirsty for righteousness. He is saying that each person grabbed hold of by Him and His gospel becomes poor in spirit, meek, merciful, and pure in heart.

To come at it from another angle, the poor in spirit are also meek. The meek are also pure in heart. The pure in heart are also merciful. The merciful also hunger and thirst for righteousness. One Beatitude flows into the next. Poverty of spirit (knowing I do not have what it takes) results in mourn-ing over the sinful condition of the world and of our own souls. Mourning gives birth to meekness, to gentleness. Gentleness creates a hunger and thirst for righteousness, which in turn produces a merciful heart, which then issues in a purity of heart. And so on.

Each Beatitude, therefore, is interpreted by the other seven. This is especially important for the seventh Beatitude, "Blessed are the peacemakers." Beatitudes one through six describe qualities of those who can make peace in our world.

---

1 I owe this insight to Martyn Lloyd-Jones (D. Martyn Lloyd-Jones, *Studies in the Sermon on the Mount, Volume 1* [Grand Rapids: Eerdmans, 1959], 34) and John Stott (John R.W. Stott, *Christian Counter-Culture: The Message of the Sermon on the Mount* [Downers Grove: InterVarsity Press, 1978], 31).

Beatitude eight describes what usually happens to those who strive for peace. Jesus is saying that those who can make peace in the world are those who know and admit their spiritual poverty; those who mourn over the violence in the world and their own heart; those who are meek, who, recognizing their powerlessness, throw themselves upon the power of God; those who hunger and thirst for right-relationship, for moral, economic, psychological, and spiritual wholeness; those who are merciful both to their allies and enemies; and those who are pure in heart.

And Jesus is saying that those who make peace get in trouble with the status quo; they meet opposition, and they may even get hurt. It happened to Peter, it happened to Paul, it happened to Jesus.

The point is, all eight Beatitudes are true of all upon whom the kingdom comes... to one degree or another. All eight are interrelated and inseparable, which means we can move the "for theirs/for they" clauses around and attach them to any of the eight "blessed are" clauses. Blessed are the meek, for they shall be comforted, and they shall receive mercy, and they shall see God. Blessed are those who mourn, for they shall be comforted, but also blessed are those who mourn, for they shall inherit the earth, and they shall be satisfied, and they shall be called children of God.

The interrelatedness of the Beatitudes is not to say that their order is unimportant! There is a sequential flow, and it all begins in poverty of spirit. The twentieth-century preacher G. Campbell Morgan said, "There is a great sequence [in the Beatitudes]. Experimentally no man [or woman] enters into any of these, save in the order indicated."[2] The fourth-century preacher John Chrysostom emphasized the orderly nature of the Beatitudes by stating:

> Therefore, you see, in each instance, by the former precept making way for the following one, He [Jesus] hath woven a sort of golden chain for us. Thus, first, he that is "humble," will surely also "mourn" for his own sins: he that so "mourns," will be both "meek," and "righteous," and "merciful;" he that is "merciful," and "righteous," and "contrite," will of course be also "pure in heart:" and such a one will be "a peacemaker" too.[3]

THE MEANING OF "BLESSED"

The word translated "blessed" is a word "crammed full of meaning."[4] The word is makarios. Although the word can be (and often is) translated as "happy," to do so is misleading. Yes, by using the term, Jesus intends to impart a certain kind of happiness to our souls. But the English word "happy" is too weak. "Happy" is related to "happening," which means that happiness comes and goes as favorable happenings come and go.

But the primary reason why "happy" is misleading is that it puts the emphasis in the wrong place. Makarios does

---

2 G. Campbell Morgan, *The Gospel According to Matthew* (London: Oliphants, n.d.), 45.

3 John Chrysostom, *Homilies on the Gospel of Matthew* in *A Select Library of the Nicene and Post-Nicene Fathers of the Christian Church, Volume 10,* ed. Philip Schaff (Grand Rapids: Wm. B. Eerdmans, 1975 reprint), 96.

4 Jones, *The Christ of the Mount*, 52.

not refer to how you and I assess ourselves or our condition; makarios refers to how God assesses us and our condition. Whether you or I feel happy is not the point of the word Jesus uses. The point is whether or not God is happy. This is not quite the way to put it, but at least it shifts the focus to where it belongs.

Now, when I realize that God is happy about me and my condition, I might then be happy. But my feeling happy is not the point. As Peter Kreeft puts it, "blessedness... is an objective state, not a subjective feeling."[5] What matters is not how I feel about me and my condition, but how God feels about me and my condition.

We need, therefore, to find a more helful synonym for "blessed." Some suggest "fortunate": "Fortunate are those who hunger and thirst for righteousness." Others suggest "approved": "Approved are those who mourn." Still others suggest "congratulations." This is getting closer, for it puts the emphasis in the right place. "Congratulations to the poor in spirit," "Congratulations to the gentle." Yet that synonym can also be misleading, suggesting that the poor in spirit and the gentle have achieved something. One synonymous phrase that I like a lot is "You lucky bums!" That captures it, doesn't it? Or, what about "Good on you!" or "God smiles on you!"

How about "right-on"? "Right-on are those who mourn." "Right-on are the merciful." "Right-on are the peacemakers." When I hear God's "right-on," I just might feel happy, but the emphasis lies where it should—with God's assessment of me and my condition.

---

5 Peter Kreeft, *For Heaven's Sake* (Nashville: Thomas Nelson, 1986), 85.

Or, what about "right-up"? Better yet, "right-side up"? "Right-side up are the poor in spirit," "Right-side up are the merciful." From the perspective of our un-kingdomized value system, the qualities Jesus blesses are upside down. "The meek inherit the earth"? Come on Jesus, be realistic. "Those who mourn are to be congratulated?" Upside down, Jesus. "No," says Jesus, "*makarios,* right-side up." The qualities He blesses only seem upside down because our old humanity is upside down. Jesus comes into the world with His kingdom and turns everything right-side up. Jesus affects what German theologian Helmut Thielicke called "the transvaluation of values."[6] "Right-side up are the gentle." "Right-side up are the pure in heart."

What about "in alignment"? Taking our car to the tire station to have the wheels aligned, I thought, "This is what Jesus is doing, realigning our reality." "'In-alignment' are the poor in spirit." "'In-alignment' are those who hunger and thirst for right-relationship."

Or, what about "in sync"? Or even "synchronized?" I think this gets at the point of *makarios* best. "In sync with the kingdom of heaven are the poor in spirit." "In sync with the kingdom of God are the merciful." "In sync with God's new world order are the pure in heart."

Again, what you or I think or feel about these qualities is not the point. The point is what God thinks or feels. In His Beatitudes, Jesus is announcing the Divine "blessed."

Makarios

Congratulations

---

6 Helmut Thielicke, *Life Can Begin Again: Sermons on the Sermon on the Mount*, trans. John W. Doberstein (London: James Clarke & Co, 1963), 77.

You lucky bums

Right-on

Right-side up

In-alignment

In sync

THE SUPERNATURAL CHARACTER OF THE BEATITUDES

The qualities that Jesus blesses are not natural human qualities. This is crucial to keep in mind when we go on to look at the Beatitudes one at a time. None of us can produce these qualities. Jesus did not come into Galilee looking for "Beatitude people" He could then call into His kingdom. No, Jesus first called ordinary, broken people to Himself and into His kingdom. As a result of contact with Him, as a result of submission to His rule, the qualities He blesses began to appear in their lives.

The first line of Jesus' Sermon on the Mount is not, "Blessed are the poor in spirit, therefore theirs is the kingdom." The first line is "Blessed are the poor in spirit, because theirs is the kingdom." It is not "In sync are the poor in spirit, therefore they get the kingdom." It is "In sync are the poor in spirit, because it is a sign that the kingdom is breaking into their lives." Not "therefore," but "because." If it were "therefore," we would try to become poor in spirit in order to get in on the kingdom, and we would end up being proud that we were humble enough to be humble. Poverty in spirit, mourning, gentleness, hungering and thirsting for righteousness, mercy, purity in heart, peacemaking, and being persecuted are all the result of the gospel breaking through to us. They are consequences of turning around and embracing the reign of Jesus Christ.

This is especially good to know regarding "pure in heart." Whatever it means, it is not the result of our own self-effort; it is the result of an ongoing encounter and ever-deepening relationship with Jesus. It is the result of being infused by His grace, the result of the kingdom breaking in and doing its re-creating work.

This does not mean that we are merely passive before Jesus, for He continually calls us to repent and believe, to turn around at ever-deeper levels and embrace Him and His reign more fully. As we do so, day after day, week after week, year after year, we are slowly but surely turned right-side up in an upside down world. We are synchronized with the really real.

The kingdom of God has come near, and a new kind of humanity is emerging in the world!

2

BEATITUDE ONE:
OH, YOU FORTUNATE PAUPERS!

MATTHEW 5:3

We were leaving the restaurant where we had been talking about Jesus' call to discipleship. "I am not going to make it," he said. "I simply do not have what it takes." He spoke in all seriousness and with a deep sense of sadness. "I see what Jesus calls me to do. He's calling me to a different kind of life. Given the massive needs all around us, how could he not? Given who He is, He has to call us beyond. I wouldn't want Him to call me to anything less. But I'm not going to make it—I just don't have what it takes."

I have good news for my friend, and for anyone who feels the way he does: Yes, you are going to make it. The problem is, you have misunderstood what Jesus is doing in His Beatitudes and the Sermon on the Mount. Given the original context in which Jesus spoke, and given the performative power of His word, we *are* going to make it. Indeed, the fact that we feel we are not going to make it says that we already are making it.

REVIEW

As I emphasized in the introductory chapter, if we separate the Beatitudes from the original context in which He first spoke them, they become either frustrating idealism or oppressive legalism. Jesus first spoke His Beatitudes right after announcing His gospel, His good news. So the question we ask again is, "What is His gospel?" What is the good news Jesus announces?

The gospel according to Jesus is the announcement of a great fact. Because of the sheer magnitude of this great fact, by necessity it impacts all other facts. The gospel according to Jesus is the announcement that in Him and because of Him, the long-awaited kingdom of heaven has come near (Matthew 4:17). As we hear Jesus say in Mark 1:15, "The time is fulfilled, and the kingdom of God is at hand; repent and believe in the gospel." The gospel according to Jesus is the announcement that history has reached a major crisis point! The future is spilling over into the present; heaven is invading the earth. Good news indeed!

And one of the clearest indications that all this is happening is the emergence of "Beatitude" people.

The first quality of such people is "poor in spirit." "Blessed are the poor in spirit, for theirs is the kingdom of heaven." I am so glad that Jesus begins on this note! I want to ask three questions of this first Beatitude:

1. What does "poor in spirit" mean?
2. Why is "poverty of spirit" a sign that the gospel is grabbing hold, that we are in sync with His in-breaking kingdom?
3. Is there ever a time when we are "rich in spirit"?

WHAT "POOR IN SPIRIT" MEANS

There are two words for "poor" in the Greek New Testament. One (*penes*) describes people who have to work all the time because they own no property. The other (*ptochoi*) describes people who are so destitute that they are forced to beg from others.[1] The first refers to those who only have the bare essentials; the second refers to those who have absolutely nothing and know it.

It is the second word (*ptochoi*) that Jesus uses in this first Beatitude. "Blessed are the destitute in spirit, the beggarly poor in spirit." Beggars come with empty hands and empty pockets; they have nothing to offer in return for food. "Congratulations," says the bringer of the kingdom of God. "Right-on," says the Savior of the world. "Right-on" are those who approach the Living God with empty hands; in sync are those who come with empty pockets. What?

The poor in spirit are those who know that they have nothing with which to get the kingdom of God. The poor in spirit are those who come totally at the mercy of the kingdom Giver. Surprise! Yours is the glorious kingdom of heaven!

Now, you may know that in the Gospel according to Luke we have a slightly different version of the first Beatitude. Or, is it that Luke records a different sermon Jesus preached, similar to the one that Matthew records? Is it that like any good teacher, Jesus taught the notion of the in-breaking kingdom on a number of occasions? Could Matthew have recorded for us a

---

1 Friedrich Hauck, s.v. *"ptochos"* in *Theological Dictionary of the New Testament*, ed. Gerhard Friedrich, trans. Geoffrey W. Bromiley (Grand Rapids: Wm B. Eerdmans, 1968), VI:886.

sermon Jesus preached on a mountainside (the Sermon on the Mount) while Luke recorded for us a sermon Jesus preached a little later on a level place (the Sermon on the Plain)?

At any rate, in Luke, Jesus says, "Blessed are the poor" (Luke 6:20). In Matthew, Jesus says, "Blessed are the poor in spirit." Many scholars ask whether Matthew has "spiritualized" Luke by adding "in spirit." Or, has Luke "socialized" Matthew by dropping "in spirit"? As I have wrestled with this over the years, I keep concluding that the two versions of the Beatitude are essentially getting at the same thing. Let me try to explain.

Throughout the Bible, we meet a God who is the Champion of the powerless. Why is Israel chosen by God as the people through whom He will bless the world? Because as Israel acknowledges, Israel was powerless before those who thought they were powerful. Throughout the Bible there seems to be a "Divine preference" for the powerless, for orphans, widows, prisoners, aliens, and the poor.

Yet nowhere in the Bible is material poverty held out to us as the ideal human condition. Nowhere in the story is the Living God happy when people are materially poor. It would be wrong to take Jesus' words in Luke to mean "it is good to be poor," and that therefore only the materially poor inherit the kingdom of God. Although Luke, more than the other Gospel writers, stresses Jesus' teaching on the poor, Luke never romanticizes or celebrates material poverty.

Why then are the poor blessed in Luke's version of Jesus' Beatitudes? Why are the poor congratulated? Why "Blessed are the poor" (period)? Because of the resultant attitude: The poor know they need help—the poor know they need God, and therefore, they live depending on God. The poor have only one hope; their whole existence hangs on God and God alone. This is why Mother Teresa enjoyed serving the poor, and it is why Jesus pronounces His "in sync" on the poor. In the Bible, the opposite of "poor" is not "rich." In the Bible the opposite of "poor" is "violent"—those who take life into their own hands.[2]

In Luke's Gospel, Jesus pronounces a woe upon the rich, not because they have much, but because of the attitude wealth produces, the attitude of not needing God, of living independently of God. The rich (and most of us reading this fall into that category) have, or think we have, other grounds for hope than the Living God—until a hurricane wipes out parts of our city, or an earthquake shakes houses to rubble, or a recession decimates pension funds! The poor are not shaken by such events, for the poor are not deceived into thinking that riches are the grounds for security for the future.

The poor do not inherit the kingdom of God because they are poor. That would be a perversion of the gospel—a kind of "salvation by social class." The poor who inherit the kingdom of God are the poor in spirit who stand before God and the world in utter helplessness.

Robert Guelich, in his work on the Sermon on the Mount, summarizes the Biblical perspective best. He works with the Aramaic word Jesus might have used, the word 'nwm, which by the first century had a particular meaning. Guelich writes:

> The poor in Judaism referred to those in desperate
> need (socio-economic element) whose helplessness

---

2 Ibid., VI:888.

drove them to a dependent relationship with God (religious element) for the supplying of their needs and vindication. Both elements are consistently present, although 'nwm does place more stress on the latter.[3]

Guelich goes on to say that "for Matthew, the poor in spirit are those who find themselves waiting, empty-handed, upon God alone for their hope and deliverance."[4]

Surprise, surprise—Jesus switches the price tags. It is the powerless, the spiritually bankrupt, and those who feel inadequate in the things of God, who experience the coming of the kingdom.

Thus, my friend Dale Bruner can say: "The Sermon on the Mount is, spiritually speaking, actually the sermon from the valley. It starts low. It starts with those who feel very unlike mountains!"[5] "Right-on," says Jesus, "in alignment," for theirs are the glorious benefits of the rule of God.

Now, as a matter of fact, all human beings are spiritually bankrupt apart from Jesus Christ. We are all spiritual paupers. No one has anything with which to buy the kingdom. However, not everyone acknowledges this universal spiritual poverty. Therefore, the poor in spirit whom Jesus blesses are those who recognize and admit their bankruptcy. The beggarly poor have laid aside all pretense; the beggarly poor have stopped playing denial games. The beggarly poor know they

---

3 Robert Guelich, *The Sermon on the Mount: A Foundation for Understanding* (Dallas: Word Publishing, 1982), 69.
4 Ibid., 75.
5 F. Dale Bruner, *The Christbook: A Historical/Theological Commentary (Matthew 1-12)* (Waco, TX: Word Books, 1987 edition), 137.

are fundamentally helpless, and they admit it. And they have Jesus' "blessed," "right-side up," "in sync."

WHY POVERTY OF SPIRIT IS A MARK OF THE GOSPELIZED

Now, I am suggesting that the qualities Jesus congratulates in His Beatitudes are not natural human qualities. Rather, they are the result of having been grabbed by His gospel. Jesus did not come into the world looking for Beatitude people He could then call into His kingdom. No, He came into the world and called people to Himself, and then, as a result of the encounter and ongoing relationship with Him, these qualities began to emerge within them.

When we encounter Jesus Christ as He really is, beyond our inadequate images of Him—when we see Him in His Glory, full of grace and truth—we see ourselves as we really are. Loved by Him, yes, with an extravagant love! But also falling short of who we were made to be. When the light of His in-breaking kingdom dawns upon us, when the Glory of His new world order is revealed to us, we become aware as never before of how far short we have fallen of the glory of God (Romans 3:23).

As Jesus said, just before going to the cross, "If I had not come and spoken to them, they would not have sin" (John 15:22). It is His presence that makes us aware of just how poor we are in the things of God. We see Him as He is and ourselves as we are, and like the tax-collector in Jesus' parable we cry out, "God, be merciful to me" (Luke 18:13).

The Pharisee in the parable could go on and on about his spiritual achievements because he was only comparing himself to other humans. And as long as we do that, we can always find someone worse off than we:

> You will find someone who is prouder than you are, and although you may still be quite proud you will congratulate yourself on being humble. You will find someone who has strong fits of temper, and although you too have a temper you will congratulate yourself on being more moderate in your temper than he.[6]

But when we are confronted by the purity and compassion, the integrity and peace of Jesus of Nazareth, the illusion breaks, and like Peter we fall at Jesus' feet and cry out, "Go away from me, Lord, for I am a sinful man!" (Luke 5:8). Peter is not suffering from a poor self-image. He has simply been arrested by the infinite qualitative difference between who he is and who he was made to be as reflected in Jesus.

It was while reading Thomas à Kempis's Imitation of Christ that John Newton, the author of "Amazing Grace," came to the blessedness of knowing his spiritual poverty. Before that encounter with Jesus, Newton was a skipper on an English slave-trading ship. He thought of himself as "quite a decent chap," thank you. Then the light broke through, and the kingdom of heaven invaded his life. And his hymn is his personal testimony:

---

6 James M. Boice, *The Sermon on the Mount: An Exposition* (Grand Rapids: Zondervan, 1972), 27.

Amazing grace, how sweet the sound
That saved a wretch like me.

"A wretch": It is his own self-designation. No one else called him that. No one needed to. In the presence of Jesus Christ, what else would a slave-trader say? He did not have a self-esteem problem. He simply saw how short of the glory of God he had fallen.

I once was lost but now am found,
Was blind but now I see.

"Now I see" that before the Living God I am woefully poor in spirit. That is why he goes on in the second verse to sing, "Twas grace that taught my heart to fear." Grace taught him to fear? Yes, for grace first makes us see ourselves as we are apart from grace. The gospel of God's new order first caused Newton to see how wretched his part in the old order was. But then he made the greatest discovery of his life. The new order, the kingdom of heaven, is for those who recognize how wretchedly poor they are before God. And so he sang, "and grace my fear relieved."

I am so glad Jesus began His description of the new humanity on this note! For every time I read the rest of the New Testament, I find myself hanging my head and wondering if I can make it; for when I listen to Jesus describe the kingdom life, I have to cry out, "O Lord, have mercy on me."

I hear "everyone who is angry with his brother (or sister) shall be guilty before the court... and whoever says, 'you fool,' shall be guilty enough to go into the fiery hell"(Matthew 5:22). I hear "everyone who looks at a woman with lust for her has already committed adultery with her in his heart" (Matthew 5:28). I hear "No one can serve two masters... You cannot serve God and wealth" (Matthew 6:24). I hear "do not be worried about your life... do not worry about tomorrow" (Matthew 6:25, 34). I hear "Do not judge so that you will not be judged... why do you look at the speck that is in your brother's eye, but do not notice the log that is in your own eye?" (Matthew 7:1, 3). And I hang my head.

I hear "let your statement be, 'Yes, yes' or 'No, no'; anything beyond this is of evil" (Matthew 5:37). I hear "do not resist an evil person; but whoever slaps you on the right cheek turn to him the other also" (Matthew 5:39). I hear "love your enemies and pray for those who persecute you" (Matthew 5:44). I hear "Not everyone who says to Me 'Lord, Lord' will enter the kingdom of heaven, but he who does the will of My Father who is in heaven" (Matthew 7:21). And I have to cry out, "O Lord, I do not have what it takes to be and do what You call me to be and do!"

And then I hear "blessed," "congratulations!" "in sync" are those who know they fall short, and who know they cannot make it on their own, for theirs and only theirs is the kingdom. It is the "in sync" who echo the words of the old hymn "Rock of Ages":

> Nothing in my hand I bring,
> Simply to the cross I cling;
> Naked, come to thee for dress;
> Helpless, look to those for grace;

Foul, I to the fountain fly;

Wash me, Savior, or I die.[7]

Brennan Manning spent most of his life as a priest before the light of the kingdom dawned on him. He suggested that the poor in spirit are like the survivors of a shipwreck. Out at sea, all the things they used to rely on—past achievements, accumulated treasures, titles and degrees—simply do not matter. All that matters now is the plank to which they cling. Manning writes:

> The shipwrecked have stood at the still-point of a turning world and discovered that the human heart is made for Jesus Christ and cannot really be content with less. They cannot take seriously the demands that the world makes on them. ... We are made for Christ and nothing less will ever satisfy us.[8]

> The shipwrecked have little in common with the landlocked. The landlocked have their own security system, a home base, credentials and credit cards, storehouses and barns, their self-interest and investments intact. They never find themselves because they never really feel themselves lost.... The shipwrecked, on the contrary, reach out for the passing plank with the desperation of the drowning. Adrift

---

7 Augustus M. Toplady, "Rock of Ages" (written 1763).
8 Brennan Manning, *Lion and Lamb: The Relentless Tenderness of Jesus* (Old Tappan, NJ: Fleming H. Revell, 1986), 178-179.

on an angry sea, in a state of utter helplessness and vulnerability, the shipwrecked never asked what they could do to merit the plank and inherit the kingdom of dry land. They knew that there was absolutely nothing any of them could do.[9]

Then Manning writes:

Like little children they simply received the plank as a gift. And little children are precisely those who haven't done anything. "Unless you... become like little children, you will never enter the kingdom of heaven" (Matthew 18:3). Jesus is not suggesting that heaven is a vast playground for infants. Children are our model because they have no claim on heaven. If they are close to God, Simon Tugwell says, "it is not because they are innocent but because they are incompetent."[10]

Blessed are the incompetent in spirit, for theirs and only theirs is the kingdom of heaven!

How do you respond to the first Beatitude? It is a kind of death, is it not? Kind of? It is death—death to self-sufficiency, death to self-saviorship. But since self-sufficiency and self-savioring are illusions, this death is actually a birth. As anyone in a twelve-step recovery program will tell us, it was when we embraced the first step ("We admitted we were powerless") that we began to be free. The poor in spirit are those who know

---

9 Ibid., 182-183.
10 Ibid., 183.

they do not have it all together. They are therefore ready to receive. They are therefore willing to receive.

WILL WE EVER BE RICH IN SPIRIT?

So, will we ever be rich in spirit? Yes and No. No, because we were created to live dependently. We will never be able to live apart from God. In the new creation we will gladly live dependent lives. As someone has said, "Even in that life there will be the need for supplies from outside ourselves. Even there, we shall not be independent of Him (God). Oh, blessed absence of self-sufficiency. We shall never be self-contained."[11] So no, we will never, on our own, be "rich in spirit."

But yes, there is a time when we are "rich in spirit"—every time we are "poor in spirit." For every time we are "poor in spirit," Jesus says to us: "yours is the kingdom." Yours! All of it! The kingdom. Everything God's glorious new world order entails is all yours: Forgiveness of sin, deep cleansing, freedom, freshness, wisdom, power, truth, hope, light, holiness, community, fullness, gifts of the Spirit, creativity—all yours.

You lucky bums! You blessed paupers!

---

11 My notes say that this is F.B. Meyer, reflecting on Revelation 22, but I have not been able to locate the source of the quotation.

3

BEATITUDE TWO
GOD'S ACHING VISIONARIES

MATTHEW 5:4

"Blessed are those who mourn." Since Jesus is using the present participle, it is more accurately, "Blessed are those who are mourning." Even more exactly, "Blessed are those who are in a state of mourning."

Really?

Jesus' second Beatitude is probably the best known and the most quoted of the eight, rivaled only by "Blessed are the peacemakers." Jesus' second Beatitude is certainly the most jarring, the one that on first hearing simply makes no sense. Blessed? Approved? Fortunate… are those who are mourning? Congratulations? Right-on? In sync are those who are in a state of mourning? Can you imagine standing before a group of people after an earthquake and repeating Jesus' words?

As J. Barrie Shepherd responds to Jesus, "Lord, you might as well say 'full are the hungry,' 'healthy are the sick,' even 'alive are the dead.'"[1] Or, as philosopher Nicholas Wolterstorff puts it in the book he wrote after the death of his 25-year-old son:

> "Blessings to those who mourn, cheers to those who weep, hail to those whose eyes are filled with tears, hats off to those who suffer, bottoms up to the grieving. How strange, how incredibly strange."[2]

What makes Jesus' second Beatitude all the more jarring is that the verb translated "mourn" (*penthein*) is one of the strongest words for grief in the Greek language. It is used of those who grieve the loss of loved ones, shedding those tears that well up from deep within our souls. It describes that piercing sorrow which issues in audible lament. As one New Testament scholar observes: "*Penthein* does not have to be open lamentation, neither is it quiet sorrow of heart. What is meant is passionate grief which leads to corresponding action."[3]

Amazing! "Blessed, right-on, in sync are those who mourn. You lucky bums!" Really? Are you sure, Jesus?

As I have been stressing thus far in this book, the qualities Jesus blesses are not natural human qualities. Rather, they are the result of the gospel having grabbed hold of us—the result of hearing Jesus' good news of the kingdom of heaven breaking in upon the earth. Jesus did not come into Galilee and Judea

---

1 J. Barrie Shepherd, *Prayers from the Mount* (Philadelphia: Westminster Press, 1986), 17.
2 Nicholas Wolterstorff, *Lament for a Son* (Grand Rapids: William B. Eerdmans, 1987), 84.
3 Rudolf Bultmann, s.v. "*penthos*," "*pentheo*" in *Theological Dictionary of the New Testament*, ed. Gerhard Friedrich, trans. Geoffrey W. Bromiley (Grand Rapids: Wm B. Eerdmans, 1968), VI:42.

looking for Beatitude people whom He could then call into the kingdom. No, He first called people to Himself. As a result of contact with Him, the Beatitudes began to emerge in their lives.

Therefore, the picture the second Beatitude suggests is not that of Jesus coming into our city, spotting people who are mourning, and reaching out to them with comfort. He did do that, blessed be His name. He spotted the widow in the town of Nain, following behind the funeral procession that was carrying her son's corpse to the cemetery, and He reached out to her (Luke 7:11-17). He saw the tears flowing down the faces of Mary and Martha as they stood outside the tomb of their brother Lazarus, and He so reached out to them that He Himself began to weep (John 11:1-37). But those encounters are not the primary picture suggested by the second Beatitude. Rather, the picture is that of Jesus coming into our city, reaching out, and calling people to Himself who then begin to mourn. Yes, they (and we) begin to rejoice deeply! But they (and we) also begin to mourn deeply.

Why? Why is piercing sorrow a sign that human beings are being grabbed by the gospel? Why does Jesus identify "passionate grief" as one of the marks of those upon whom the light dawns, upon whom the kingdom of God has come?

PRELIMINARY OBSERVATIONS

Before wrestling with the question, let us realize what it means for us that Jesus actually blesses grieving.

Right off, this Beatitude gives us permission to grieve; it allows us the freedom to grieve. North America and parts of the world under Western influence need to hear this—for we are not free to grieve, even in many Christian circles. A wife breaks down in the middle of the memorial service for her husband of forty years, and from the back pew is heard, "Too bad, I really thought she would be strong." Jesus would never say that! Never. He Himself was overcome by passionate grief, and He Himself openly expressed His grief. Who says that "big boys don't cry"? Not Jesus, a man's man. He gives us the freedom and space to grieve.

I think Jesus is also saying in this Beatitude that we will not know the comfort He gives unless we let ourselves grieve. He is saying to us, "Comfort is found when you allow yourself to feel and express grief." I have walked through "the valley of the shadow of death" with many people. I have conducted nearly four hundred memorial services. And I have observed that those who go through the valley most redemptively are those who do not try to stifle their grief. Grief does not kill. It feels like it will, but it does not. It is trying to suppress the grief that kills. Jesus is saying to us, "Comfort is not found by insulating your heart but by opening your heart." One of the ways we can serve one another is by encouraging one another to grieve better.

Jesus' blessing of grieving is also His way of letting us know right from the beginning that living in His kingdom in the world will involve sorrow. He does not promise us unbroken happiness. Yes, there is great joy. Joy springs from the pages of the New Testament. "The time is fulfilled!"—Rejoice. "The kingdom of God has come near!"—Rejoice. "The Lover of our souls is here in our midst!"—Rejoice. "Our God reigns!"—

Rejoice. "The Holy Spirit is here!"—Rejoice. Yet Jesus is saying that His coming also brings sorrow, heart-piercing sorrow.

And when Jesus blesses our grieving, it is His way of telling us that this sorrow is part of the process by which we grow. As Christian counselor Keith Krull said to me one day as we were talking about the Beatitudes, "Sadness is a launching pad to growth." There are times as we minister to one another when we try to anaesthetize one another's sorrow too quickly. C.S. Lewis observed, "God whispers to us in our pleasure, speaks in our conscience, but shouts in our pains: it is His megaphone to rouse a deaf world."[4] We need to listen to our pain, our sorrow, and our sadness, for it may be one of the ways that God is maturing us.

"Blessed are those who mourn." Why? Why is mourning a sign that human beings have been grabbed by the gospel? Why is passionate grief a sign that Jesus and His kingdom are getting a hold on us?

I know of three reasons.

THE REALITY OF SIN

The first reason is related to what we realized from the first Beatitude, "Blessed are the poor in spirit." When we meet Jesus in all His fullness, we are forced to face the reality of sin, especially the reality of sin in our own lives. Not that Jesus walks into our lives and tells us that we are "sinners"! Not at all—nowhere in the gospel do we find Jesus telling someone that he or she is a "sinner."

---

4 C.S. Lewis, *The Problem of Pain* (New York: MacMillan Publishing, 1962), 93.

It is just that in His presence, we cannot but realize our sinful condition. This is part of the reason we resist deeper intimacy with Him: We are afraid of what He will do with what is exposed in His presence. In Him we see what humanity was created to be. And when we see what we were created to be, we grieve over what humanity has become because of the power of sin.

What was the apostle Paul's response to Jesus, even after years of walking with Him? "Wretched man that I am! Who will set me free from the body of this death?" (Romans 7:24). Paul is not suffering from low self-esteem. He is wrestling with the fact that even though he knows what is good, and even though he wills to do what he knows is good, he keeps doing the very evil he does not will (Romans 7:19). Do you identify with that? I do! There are times when I am appalled by the depth of my capacity to go against what I know to be the will of God. In the presence of Jesus, we see and rejoice and mourn. Is the 1928 version of the Anglican Prayer Book over-reaching when it has worshippers say, "We acknowledge and bewail our manifold sins and wickedness"?

This is not "worm theology," the theology that says that in order to know God we have to first feel like a worm, and squirm and wriggle in the mud for a while. God does not think of us as worms! Jesus never called anyone "worm."[5] The second Beatitude is not advocating a "put-yourself-down" spirituality. It is simply recognizing that in the presence of Jesus the Holy

---

5 He did call some Pharisees "snakes" (Matthew 23:33), but never "worms."

One, we cannot but grieve over our unholy condition. In His presence we rejoice, but we also grieve.

The wonder of the gospel is that the Holy One chooses to draw near to us, to draw us near to Himself, and to live among us unholy ones—indeed to live in us unholy ones! The wonder is that He does not wait until we are holy before He comes. He comes in all His Holiness into our unholiness, our unholiness is automatically exposed, and we grieve.

"Blessed," He says. "Blessed are those who so grieve." Right-on. It means the Holy One has a hold on you! It means you are in sync with the really real. It means you are alive.

DRAWING NEAR TO JESUS' HEART

A second reason why mourning is a sign the gospel is breaking through is that as we get closer to Jesus we get closer to His heart, and we discover that it is a broken heart. Oh yes, Jesus is a man of joy! So much so that He was accused by stuffy religious folk of being a glutton and a drunkard. But He is, as the prophet Isaiah says, "a man of sorrow, acquainted with grief" (Isaiah 53:4). Yes, He is the eternally joyful Creator, who out of infinite joy creates us to enter into His joy. The psalmist is right—"In Your presence is fullness of joy; In Your right hand there are pleasures forever" (Psalm 16:11). But there is in His heart, because of the destructive power of sin, great sorrow over the world and over the church. How often throughout scripture do we find the phrase "and it grieved the Holy One"?

Matthew tells us that when Jesus saw the multitudes bringing their sick to Him, He "felt compassion for them" (Matthew 9:35-36). The word is *splankna*, guts. That Jesus

49

"felt compassion for them" means "His guts were ripped up." That too is the wonder of the gospel. The Living God chooses to so enter all the wreckage that He feels it Himself—He feels it as His own.

John tells us that Jesus wept at the grave of Lazarus (John 11:35). The word John uses means a spontaneous out-breaking, an uncontrollable weeping. Jesus stands alongside the grave of His good friend, and tears roll down His face. Why? Because of the pain He could feel in the hearts of Lazarus's sisters, Mary and Martha. And because of the pain He Himself was feeling. The tears are the overflow of the Creator's broken heart, saying, "Death ought not be." Get close to that heart and we cannot but be moved in the same way.

Luke tells us that as Jesus came into Jerusalem on Palm Sunday, He wept over the city (Luke 19:41). The word Luke uses is a strong word that describes a chest heaving with "the sob and the cry of a soul in agony."[6] Why? Jesus is the Sovereign King of Glory. Why would He sob? After regaining His composure, He explains that it is because they did not know the things that make for peace (Luke 19:42; see also 13:34). Get close to that heart and feel what it feels for the world, and you cannot but mourn with Him.

GRIEVING OVER WHAT IS

The third reason why mourning is a sign that the gospel is breaking through: In Jesus, we see what the kingdom of God is all about, what God's new world order is all about. In Jesus

---

6 G. Campbell Morgan, *The Gospel According to Luke* (New York: Fleming H. Revell, 1931), 221.

we see what was supposed to be, and what will be when the kingdom comes in all its fullness. And we grieve over what is. As Dietrich Bonhoeffer puts it, the disciples of Jesus "see that for all the jollity on board, the ship is beginning to sink."[7]

Oh, disciples do begin to see signs of the kingdom in our midst. Yet the more we see of what can be, the more our hearts break over what is.

I look over the city where I live and work, and my heart wants to cry out, "It does not have to be this way." The poor do not have to go on being poor. There is enough to go around. Jesus' Father has seen to that. It is just that the systems of distribution are so unjust. The world does not have to spend trillions of dollars a year building weapons, astronomically more than what we spend on health, education, and social services combined. It does not have to be this way. Domestic quarrels do not have to end in violence; there are many other steps to take before grabbing a knife or a gun. Racial tensions do not have to continue. We can find ways to overcome prejudice and suspicion. The environment does not have to be abused. We can change our driving habits if we want to. We can change the way we package goods if we want to. We can find better ways of disposing toxic chemicals if we want to. Women and children do not have to go on being sexually exploited. Those profiting from prostitution and pornography—violence against women—make grossly huge sums of money. It does not have

---

7 Dietrich Bonhoeffer, *The Cost of Discipleship*, rev. ed. (New York: Mac-Millan Publishing, 1959), 121.

to be this way. Women should not be treated this way: 92% of the women being prostituted want out.[8]

All of this is, of course, symptomatic of the deeper spiritual crisis of our time, the crisis of the lack of knowing God. Billions of people on our planet go about their daily lives, most in "quiet desperation" unaware of the great fact of Jesus and His kingdom. It does not have to be this way. Every person ought to know the good news. The "harvest is plentiful," says Jesus, "but the laborers are few," too few (Luke 10:2). It does not have to be this way.

Earlier I quoted philosopher Nicholas Wolterstorff. A number of years ago he and his wife lost their 25-year-old son, Eric, in a mountain climbing accident. In his book *Lament for a Son*, Wolterstorff openly shares his grief, agonizing over the way the world is, in light of the way the world is supposed to be. In the chapter where he reflects on Jesus' second Beatitude, he asks, "Who then are the mourners" that Jesus blesses? Wolterstorff answers:

> The mourners are those who have caught a glimpse of God's new day, who ache with all their being for that day's coming, and who break out into tears when confronted with its absence. They are the ones who realize that in God's realm of peace there is no one blind, and who ache whenever they see someone unseeing. They are the ones who realize that in

---

8 Melissa Farley, Isin Baral, Merab Kiremire, Ufuk Sezgin, "Prostitution in Five Countries: Violence and Post-Traumatic Stress Disorder," *Feminism & Psychology* 8, no. 4 (1998): 405-426.

God's realm there is no one hungry and who ache whenever they see someone starving. They are the ones who realize that in God's realm there is no one falsely accused and who ache whenever they see someone imprisoned unjustly. They are the ones who realize that in God's realm there is no one who fails to see God and who ache whenever they see someone unbelieving. They are the ones who realize that in God's realm there is no one who suffers oppression and who ache whenever they see someone beat down. They are the ones who realize that in God's realm there is no one without dignity and who ache whenever they see someone treated with indignity. They are the ones who realize that in God's realm of peace there is neither death nor tears and who ache whenever they see someone crying tears over death. The mourners are aching visionaries.[9]

"Blessed," says Jesus. "Your aching shows you are in sync with My gospel. Your aching says you are alive in My vision for the world."

YOU SHALL BE COMFORTED

"Blessed… for you shall be comforted." When? When are the mourners to receive comfort?

In the end, when the kingdom of heaven is fully realized. When, as the Voice from the throne of the universe says, God "will wipe away every tear from their eyes; and there will no

---

9 Wolterstorff, *Lament for a Son*, 85-86.

longer be any death; there will no longer be any mourning, or crying, or pain" (Revelation 21:4).

But we shall also be comforted before the end, even now. How? The word translated "comfort" is the verb *parakaleo*, a rich word. The primary meaning of *parakaleo* is to exhort, to encourage, or to embolden. It is used of soldiers cheering each other on. This is also the original meaning of the English word "comfort": *com* "with," *fortis* "strength"—com-fort, "strengthen by being with."

Jesus is saying that as we dare to open ourselves up to pain and grief, we feel ourselves strangely strengthened.

How? Why? From the verb *parakaleo* comes the noun *paraklete*. *Paraklete* is the word Jesus uses for the Holy Spirit, with whom and in whom Jesus baptized His disciples. Before the end, when every tear is wiped away, the Paraklete, the personal embodiment of the kingdom, comes alongside those who are mourning.

When we become aware of the depth of sin, the Paraklete speaks His word of comfort: "Jesus paid it all. Your guilt is removed, your iniquity is forgiven, your sin is covered by the blood of the Lamb."

When we feel just how broken the world is, the Paraklete speaks His word of comfort: He reminds us that even now the Father and the Son are at work, that creation is groaning only because it is in the throes of childbirth, that the turmoil in the world is due in part to the kingdom invading and disturbing the status quo.

When we feel despair over how far we are from the kingdom's way, the Paraklete speaks His word of comfort: The kingdom has come near; the kingdom is breaking in all over the world, and nothing can ultimately stand in its way.

As you can probably tell, I have great vision of what can be. This means that I am regularly hit by sorrow over what is. Sometimes I want to say, "Take the vision away, it would be easier not to see what can be." It is then that I sense the Paraklete speaking to my soul: "The vision is true—it does not have to be this way. Things can change. Do not carry this weight— the weight of making the vision come to be—on your own shoulders. Trust Jesus. Trust the Father." And I hear the word the Spirit spoke to the prophet Habakkuk:

> The vision is yet for the appointed time;
> It hastens toward the goal and it will not fail.
> Though it tarries, wait for it;
> For it will certainly come,
> it will not delay (Habakkuk 2:3).

When we feel the broken heart of God, the Paraklete assures us that it is the heart of God. And therefore, what God says to us is also true for Him: "Weeping may last for the night, but a shout of joy comes in the morning" (Psalm 30:5). God will have His way! Everlasting joy will be the everlasting state of being for you and me, and for God.

If the first Beatitude blesses those who are poor before God and who own their utter helplessness, the second Beatitude blesses those who are vulnerable before life and who dare to feel its pain. Theirs is the kingdom, and theirs is the embrace of the God of all comfort.

4

BEATITUDE THREE
THE INVINCIBLE

MATTHEW 5:5

"Blessed are the meek, for they shall inherit the earth."
You lucky bums! Really? You're sure about this, Jesus?

WHAT MEEKNESS IS NOT

We need to get two things straight right from the beginning. First, the quality Jesus blesses in the third Beatitude has nothing to do with all the negative images triggered by the English word "meek." Although it is a challenge to pin down the exact meaning of the original word Jesus uses, it clearly does not mean no brain, no brawn, no backbone; it clearly does not mean no convictions, no courage, no spirit, no drive, no guts.

How do we know this? For one simple reason: Only two people in the Bible are explicitly described by the word Jesus uses in His Beatitude—Moses and Jesus. Hardly wimps!

In the Old Testament book of Numbers, we read about Moses, who led the great exodus of the Jews from Egypt: "Now the man Moses was very humble [meek], more than any man who was on the face of the earth" (Numbers 12:3). And in the Gospel according to Matthew, where Jesus calls us to come and take up His yoke, Jesus says of Himself, "for I am gentle [meek] and humble in heart" (Matthew 11:29). If of all the players in the great drama of salvation, Moses and Jesus alone are called by this term, then it cannot mean spinelessness. We can be sure right from the beginning that the third Beatitude is NOT "Blessed are the doormats, for they shall inherit the earth; blessed are the wimps, for they shall inherit the earth."

Now, although only Moses and Jesus are explicitly called meek in the Bible, one other player in God's salvation drama speaks of meekness more than any other: the apostle Paul. In nine different places in his letters, he either is seeking to live in meekness himself or is calling others to live in meekness. For example: "Now I, Paul, myself urge you by the meekness and gentleness of Christ" (2 Corinthians 10:1). He calls us to walk in a manner worthy of the calling with which we have been called "with all humanity and gentleness [meekness]" (Ephesians 4:2). "So, as those who have been chosen of God, holy and beloved, put on a heart of compassion, kindness, humility, gentleness [meekness] and patience" (Colossians 3:12). In Galatians 5:22-23, he lists the "fruit of the Spirit"—love, joy, peace, patience, kindness, goodness, faithfulness, gentleness [meekness], and self-control. And he speaks of meekness in many other texts (1 Corinthians 4:21; Galatians 6:1; 1 Timothy 6:11; 2 Timothy 2:25; Titus 3:2).

Paul never explicitly says anything like "I am meek and I am gentle." But this is what he seeks to be. I think he does not explicitly say, "I am meek" because he does not feel worthy of echoing Jesus' own words.

So, if Moses, Jesus, and Paul are the ones in the Bible of whom the word "meek" can be used, we can be sure the word does not mean all the negative things conjured up by the English word "meek."

Then what does it mean? What is this quality Jesus blesses and embodies? What does it mean to be meek like Moses and Paul and Jesus? And why is this a sign that Jesus and His gospel are getting hold of us? Why is meekness a sign that the kingdom of God is breaking into our lives?

THE STRENGTH OF THE PROMISE

The second thing to get straight right from the beginning is that the promise Jesus makes ("they shall inherit the earth") is rock-solid. We can put our weight on this promise.

Why? For one simple reason: the meek [singular], the meek One Himself, will inherit the earth! Jesus Christ, the meek One, will inherit the earth. After all, He made the earth! He owns the earth—always has, and always will. Psalm 24:1 tells us that "the earth is the LORD's and all it contains, the world, and those who dwell in it." The earth belongs to the Lord Jesus. I know the affirmation can be offensive in our pluralistic culture. But to be faithful to the Biblical witness to Jesus, we can say nothing less. The earth is His, which is why we either do it Jesus' way or it does not work. The Lord Jesus Christ will inherit His earth, so this outrageous promise that the meek [plural] will inherit the earth is rock solid. Those who belong to Him will inherit the earth with Him. The only questions are when, and in what sense?

So, let us dig deeper into Jesus' seemingly upside down Beatitude. As I have been emphasizing, the qualities Jesus blesses, or congratulates, in His Beatitudes are not natural human qualities. No one is naturally meek. Rather, we become meek by the power of Jesus' gospel. So why is being meek a sign that Jesus and His gospel are getting a hold on us?

MEEKNESS: BEING LIKE JESUS

The most immediate answer lies in the fact that Jesus Himself is meek. "Take my yoke upon you, and learn from Me, for I am gentle [meek]" (Matthew 11:29). When we encounter Jesus, when we embrace His embrace and receive His life, we start to become like Him. This is why the apostle Paul includes meekness in his list of the fruit of the Spirit. When Jesus infuses us with His life, with His Spirit, we begin to take on His character traits.

You can see then that there is a sense in which, in His Beatitudes, Jesus is giving us a portrait of Himself. He is poor in spirit, living in utter dependence on His Father. He hungers and thirsts for justice. He is merciful and pure in heart. And He is meek.

And, if we live with Him, we slowly become like Him. His gospel ("the kingdom of God has come near") gets hold of us and something happens. We become meek. Why?

In order to answer that question we need to investigate the meaning of the term that Jesus uses, *praeis*. Some first-century folks used the word to describe domesticated animals. Such animals had learned to accept the control of their masters. By extension, the word refers to people who know how to behave, who graciously cooperate with proper authority. Following this line, one scholar would render Jesus' words as "blessed are God's gentlemen, blessed are God's gentlewomen."[1]

The philosopher Aristotle taught that meekness was to be highly desired. He described it as a mean between anger and indifference, as the middle ground between excessive anger on the one hand and the inability to show anger at all on the other. Taking his cue from Aristotle, William Barclay renders Jesus' words, "Blessed is the man who is always angry at the right time, and never angry at the wrong time."[2] Oh to be so meek!

MEEKNESS IN PSALM 37

What has helped me most in understanding this word is looking at how it is used in other places in the Bible. Of particular help has been Psalm 37. Psalm 37 is best known for the great promise, "Delight yourself in the LORD; and He will give you the desires of your heart" (37:4). In Psalm 37:11 we read, "But the humble [or meek, or gentle] will inherit the land."

Is Jesus echoing and expanding on this Psalm in His third Beatitude? Many scholars think so, going on to argue that Psalm 37 gives us the fullest interpretation of the word "meek." Commentator Derek Kidner says of Psalm 37, "There is no

1 Boice, *The Sermon on the Mount: An Exposition,* 37.
2 William Barclay, *The Gospel of Matthew: Volume 1 (Chapters 1 to 10),* rev. ed. (Philadelphia: Westminster Press, 1975), 96.

finer exposition of the third Beatitude than this psalm from which it is drawn."[3]

The whole psalm appears to be linked together by the recurring phrase "shall inherit the land" or "shall inherit the earth."

Verse 9 –   For evildoers will be cut off;
              but those who wait for the LORD, they
              will inherit the land.

Verse 22 – For those blessed by Him will inherit the
              land, but those cursed by Him will be
              cut off.

Verse 29 – The righteous will inherit the land and
              dwell in it forever.

Verse 34 – Wait for the LORD and keep His way,
              and He will exalt you to inherit the land;

And then there's verse 11, the verse Jesus works with: "But the humble/meek will inherit the land."

Now, it is important to understand where David (the author of the psalm) is coming from when he composes Psalm 37. He is wrestling with the age-old problem of the apparent success of those who ignore and disobey God. He is wrestling with the fact that in this world it is the pushy, grabby, power-wielding, self-asserting, controlling types who seem to win.

David frankly acknowledges that the dishonest do often have more than the honest, and that those who step on others

---

3 Derek Kidner, *Psalms 1-72: An Introduction and Commentary on Books I and II of the Psalms* (Downers Grove: InterVarsity Press, 1973), 148.

do regularly get to the top. The rich often do buy their way out of the consequences of their sin. Yet in the face of all this, David makes the daring claim, which Jesus repeats with His own authority, that "the meek will inherit the land." Contrary to all appearances, the gentle will win.

In the verses before and after that claim in verse 11, David develops the nature of this meekness. He looks at it from many angles, describing it in terms of what the meek do and do not do. The meek trust in the LORD (vs 3), do good in the face of evil (vs 3), cultivate faithfulness (or trust) (vs 3), delight themselves in the LORD (vs 4), rest in the LORD (vs 7), and wait patiently for Him (vs 7). Clearly meekness is not a passive quality.

Furthermore, the meek do not fret because of evildoers (vs 1), do not envy (vs 1), cease from anger and forsake wrath (vs 8), and depart from evil (vs 27). Clearly, meekness is also not a spineless quality, for it takes great strength to cease from anger!

Let us take some time and reflect a bit more on some of David's insights.

The meek "Trust in the LORD, and do good" (vs 3). Others may get away with doing evil and with ignoring justice. But the gentle bank on doing the will of God... come what may. The gentle trust not themselves, nor their ability to orchestrate, but God. As a friend of mine puts it, "They do the Godly thing and let the chips fly."[4]

---

4 Dr. David Worth, pastor of Beverly Hills Presbyterian Church in Los Angeles.

The meek delight themselves in the LORD (vs 4). That is, they have a special focus in life. Instead of focusing on the fact that they are being taken advantage of, or do not have as much as the next person, they find their joy in the Living God. The word David uses for "delight" relates to the word "Eden." The meek find their great pleasure in the LORD, their Eden, Yahweh Himself. The gentle deliberately redirect their emotions to find peace and wholeness in a Person.[5] They find their identity and security in the very center of the universe. Oh to so live!

The meek commit their way to the LORD (vs 5). The word translated "commit" literally means "roll." They roll their way into the LORD. I like the image the verb suggests. Stuart Briscoe says:

> The meek roll their lives, their cares, their reputations onto the Lord and let the Lord worry about it all. The meek are those who, when offended, commit their wounded egos and the one offending their ego, to the Perfect Judge. The meek can say to herself, "What she did to me was wrong. But she is answerable to God, so I'll let God deal with her. But I am answerable to God, too. So I'm going to concentrate on doing right by her."[6]

The right thing may be to forgive, confront, or both, but either way, the gentle "roll it all" onto their Lord.

---

5 Kidner, *Psalms 1-72*, 149.
6 My notes indicate that this is from Stuart Briscoe, but I have not been able to locate the source.

The meek "rest in the LORD and wait patiently for Him" (vs 7). In Scripture, waiting is not a passive activity. Waiting requires great concentration and readiness to move. The sense is to "wait expectantly" on tiptoe, expecting the just God to vindicate and satisfy. Such waiting calls for confidence that God will act; such waiting calls for courage not to act too quickly. The meek have somehow come to great trust in the sovereignty of God, and in that trust they can rest. Oh to know what the meek know!

The meek "do not fret" (vs 1). Literally the word means "do not get heated."[7] The meek do not "get hot under the collar." What great strength! How many of us waste enormous amounts of energy and time, stewing over people who offend us or take advantage of us or ignore us? The meek acknowledge their emotional response to all that; they own their emotions. They manage their energy, channeling it in responsive directions.

The meek do good in the face of evil (vs 3). The meek "depart from evil" (vs 27). This is David's key insight, which Jesus more fully unfolds in the rest of His Sermon on the Mount. The meek do not return evil for evil, for they know that that is utter weakness. They do not respond to violence and injustice with more twisting of justice.

I trust you can see from this survey of Psalm 37 that the meek Jesus blesses are the "invincible meek." What can finally undo them? The meek are strong because they rest in the arms of God. The meek are wise because they look at life through the eyes of God. The meek can stand firmly because they are anchored to the Eternal. Oh to be what Jesus blesses!

---

7 Kidner, *Psalms 1-72*, 148.

MEEKNESS IN ACTION

We see all this played out in Moses. "Very humble [meek]," says the text, "more than any man who was on the face of the earth" (Numbers 12:3). Recall the specific context in which Moses is called "very meek": One day his sister Miriam and brother Aaron challenged his position within the community, and they did it publicly! In the Middle East, this was a very shameful thing to do. They did not like the woman Moses had married—and they criticized her publicly. They were jealous that Moses alone spoke God's word to God's people—and said so publicly. This was very shameful in a shame-based culture.

Has anything like that ever happened to you? It has happened to me a number of times. Several years ago, I led a weekend retreat for a group of church members. We worked our way through the apostle Paul's letter to the Colossians, and we had a great time! At the closing of the last teaching session I asked, "Is this not good news?" and I invited feedback. All of a sudden, as though he had been waiting for the opportunity to arise, a man within the group said in great anger, "No, it is not good news… it is so much blankety-blank. And furthermore you are nuts to believe it and you are ruining our fellowship with your teachings." And he lit into me for what felt like ten minutes, saying all kinds of awful things about me, all in front of the other people at the retreat.

What did Moses do that day when he got hurt? He refused to lash back at Miriam and Aaron. He refused to judge them for their insolence; he refused to get all worked up about it. No small miracle! What he did was "roll it all" on God. He knew God had called him to that leadership role. He knew God was just and would vindicate the truth of the situation. Is that being spineless? Is that being gutless? In such confrontations, it takes great strength and courage not to react in kind, not to play tit-for-tat, not to echo the attacker's spirit and words.

Do we not see all that Psalm 37 says about the meek lived out in Jesus, especially during His trial (Matthew 26-27; John 18-19)? The local police spat on Him, they blindfolded Him and hit Him in the face. The foreign military personnel repeated the insults and violence—they thrust a crown on thorns onto His skull, put a royal purple robe on Him, and mocked Him. Then they too spat on him and hit Him again and again.

But He refused to respond in kind. He did not echo their spirit and actions. As the apostle Peter (who witnessed the scenes!) later said, "while being reviled He did not revile in return; while suffering, He uttered no threats" (1 Peter 2:23). Instead, says Peter, Jesus "kept entrusting Himself to Him who judges righteously."

Roman soldiers knew power when they saw it. One of the soldiers stationed at the cross was overcome with awe at the way Jesus handled all the evil, saying, "Truly this man was the Son of God" (Mark 15:39).

Oh to have the strength to be meek! Oh to have the maturity of Jesus to be so gentle!

MEEKNESS: A SIGN OF THE NEW ORDER

Back to the question, why? Why is this quality a sign of being grabbed hold of by Jesus and His gospel? For one single reason: When the gospel breaks through, we realize the great open secret, the mystery of history: "The time is fulfilled; the kingdom of God has come near."

Those grabbed by the gospel realize that in the birth, life, death, and resurrection of Jesus of Nazareth a revolution is taking place: The old order of things is on the way out, the new order of things is on the way in. The old order of pushing, grabbing, and demanding is over. It is now collapsing in on itself. We can see it all over the world. The old order is dying. This is why it takes so much energy to make the old order work; it is like trying to pump life into a corpse. As the apostle John says, "the world is passing away, and also its lusts" (1 John 2:17). Why then, ask those who know the gospel, should we fret? Why should we play the game by the rules of a dying order?

Furthermore, those grabbed by Jesus and His gospel know the outcome of living by the old order. In Psalm 37:13, David says that God laughs at the schemes of the arrogant and dishonest. "God sees their day coming," says David. David is not referring to some calamities God will bring on them, but to the natural consequences of old-order decisions and practices. Those who get to the top by stepping on others last only until the next group of steppers step on them. Those who seize and hold power unjustly eventually fall under the weight of their own injustice. Empires built in greed are eventually eaten up by greed. Those grabbed by Jesus' gospel have seen the light and can therefore resist the inherently self-destructive ways of the old order.

To put it more simply, they have seen the preview, and they know how the movie ends. They know how it all comes out. They know the old order will be swallowed up by Jesus' new order. They believe the Hallelujah chorus—"The kingdom of the world has become the kingdom of our Lord and of His Christ; and He will reign forever and ever" (Revelation 11:15). Why then act according to the old order? To do so is foolish and futile.

Blessed, right-on, in sync are the meek, for they shall inherit the earth.

Inherit the earth? When? In the End, when the earth is fully redeemed.

But they also inherit the earth before the End—now. Who are the people who really enjoy the earth? Those who grab and push and demand? No! They are too busy grabbing and pushing and demanding to enjoy what they get by grabbing and pushing and demanding. Those who live delighting in God and delighting in God's great plans are free to smell the roses along the way.

The meek inherit the earth ahead of the End in another sense. Before he became our son, Alex was an orphan in Moscow and had nothing. But the moment he was adopted, all we had was at his disposal. The moment you and I are adopted by the Father of the Lord Jesus Christ, all God's wealth becomes ours. "All things belong to you, and you belong to Christ and Christ belongs to God" (1 Corinthians 3:22). To belong to

Jesus Christ is to be granted the privilege of living in the palace with Him, playing with His toys and enjoying His backyard. The earth is the Lord's, and He gives it to His own.

Does meek mean weak—no brain, no brawn, no back-bone? No spirit, no energy, no drive? No way! It is through the meek that the world gets turned right-side up!

> *"Rejoice greatly, O daughter of Zion!*
> *Shout in triumph, O daughters of Jerusalem!*
> *Behold, your king is coming to you.*
> *He is just and endowed with salvation,*
> *Humble [Meek], and mounted on a donkey. ...*
> *And He will speak peace to the nations;*
> *And His dominion will be from sea to sea,*
> *and from the River to the ends of the earth."*
> *(Zechariah 9:9-10)*

5

BEATITUDE FOUR
ALIVE IN A GOD-SIZED CRAVING

MATTHEW 5:6

Jesus of Nazareth comes into the towns and cities of first-century Palestine announcing what he calls the gospel of God. Here it is again: "The time is fulfilled, and the kingdom of God is at hand" (Mark 1:15).

It is time! It is time for the future to spill over into the present.[1] It is time for heaven to invade earth! In Jesus, the kingdom of light is breaking into the kingdom of darkness. In Jesus, the kingdom of justice is breaking into the kingdom of oppression. In Jesus, the kingdom of life is invading and displacing the kingdom of death!

Are we surprised that Jesus follows the announcement of this good news with the call to "repent and believe"? ... to "turn around and put your weight on the gospel"? What else can He say? "It is time. God's new world order has come near: Make a U-turn in the road and throw yourselves on me!"

---

1 George Eldon Ladd, *The Presence of the Future: The Eschatology of Biblical Realism* (Grand Rapids: William B. Eerdmans, 1974).

And when we do, something happens. A new kind of humanity begins to emerge, a new kind of humanity that Jesus is describing in the collection of sayings we call "the Beatitudes."

"Blessed are those who hunger and thirst for righteousness, for they shall be satisfied" (Matthew 5:6).

In this fourth Beatitude, Jesus draws us into what will be the major theme of the rest of His Sermon on the Mount. Indeed in this fourth Beatitude, Jesus draws us into the major theme of what it means to be human.

"Blessed, right-on, in sync with the really real are those who hunger and thirst for righteousness, for they and they alone shall be satisfied."

Let us first make sure we are hearing Jesus clearly. In His fourth Beatitude, Jesus is not saying, "Blessed are those who feel righteous." Jesus is not here saying, "Blessed are those who are on their way to being righteous"—although that is something He could say in certain contexts. Jesus is not saying, "Blessed are those who are declared righteous"—although that is something He can say in light of His work on the cross. Jesus is here saying, "Blessed are those who, although knowingly unrighteous, are hungry and thirsty for righteousness. They, and they alone, shall be filled."

THE SUPERNATURAL CHARACTER OF THE BEATITUDE

As I have been suggesting so far, the qualities Jesus congratulates in His Beatitudes are not natural human qualities. That is, we do not and cannot produce them. I cannot all of a sudden decide to become poor in spirit, or gentle, or pure in heart; I cannot decide to hunger and thirst for righteousness. Rather, the qualities Jesus congratulates come into being by the life-giving power of His goodness—they emerge in us when Jesus and His gospel of the kingdom grab hold of us.

Jesus walks into our lives and calls us to follow Him. By His grace, He causes His kingdom, His reign, to break in... and something happens. We become poor in spirit, we begin to mourn in a whole new way, and we begin to hunger and thirst as never before. We begin to crave as never before.

In Jesus, God with us, we begin to taste God's new world order. As a result we become painfully aware of how far short we have fallen; we realize our spiritual bankruptcy and utter helplessness. And then, because of what we experience in Jesus, we hunger and thirst as never before. We begin to crave with a God-sized craving.

I need to be more precise at this point. When I said that the qualities Jesus blesses in the Beatitudes are not natural human qualities, I mean that they are not natural qualities for humanity-under-the-reign-of-sin. I need to make this clarification because, as a matter of fact, we were originally created to naturally long for righteousness. I have not yet said what is meant by "righteousness," but we were hard-wired to desire righteousness.

Sadly, sin entered the picture, and sadly, we gave in to its power. Sadly, that natural human longing got twisted and distorted. And in the mix, all other natural human longings also got twisted and distorted and became more dominant. Now more than righteousness, we crave food and drink, comfort and pleasure, wealth and fame. Need I illustrate?

In His fourth Beatitude, Jesus is announcing good news. He comes into our lives, enters into all our hungers and thirsts, and restores in us the hunger and thirst for which we were made. In the process, He heals all the other natural cravings that the power of sin has twisted, some into addictions. The Savior of the world causes His kingdom to break into our worlds, and He re-wires our distorted hungers and thirsts.

The hunger and thirst for righteousness does not displace the hunger and thirst for food or drink. How could it, given that we are physical creatures who need physical sustenance? However, the hunger and thirst for righteousness does heal the hunger and thirst for food and drink by delivering it from compulsiveness. The hunger and thirst for righteousness does not negate the hunger and thirst for sexual intimacy, but it heals that deep hunger and thirst by delivering us from obsession. The hunger and thirst for righteousness does not kill the hunger and thirst for greatness, but it delivers it from ego-centrality, and thus heals it. Jesus comes and reforms our appetites.

"Blessed (in sync) are those who hunger and thirst for righteousness, for they and only they shall be satisfied."

THE RELATIONAL NATURE OF RIGHTEOUSNESS

There is no way we can exaggerate the place righteousness has in the Biblical Story—we encounter it everywhere in the Bible. In Genesis, in Exodus, in Deuteronomy (hugely), and in the Psalms:

> "His righteousness endures forever" (Psalm 111:3; 112:3, 9).

> "He guides me in the paths of righteousness for His name's sake" (Psalm 23:4).

> "Righteousness and justice are the foundation of Your throne" (Psalm 89:14).

> "The heavens declare His righteousness" (Psalm 50:6; 97:6).

> "Your righteousness is like the mountains of God" (Psalm 36:6).

We encounter it in Proverbs, in the Prophets, and in the letters of the apostle Paul. His magnum opus, his letter to the Romans, is packed with righteousness.

And it is everywhere in the teaching and preaching of Jesus. The whole Sermon on the Mount is crafted around "righteousness":

> "Unless your righteousness surpasses that of the scribes and Pharisees" (Matthew 5:20).

> "Beware of practicing your righteousness before men to be noticed by them" (Matthew 6:1).

"Seek first His kingdom and His righteousness" (Matthew 6:33).

"Blessed are those who have been persecuted for the sake of righteousness" (Matthew 5:10).

So what does "righteousness" mean? What are we dealing with here?

Old Testament scholar Gerhard von Rad has, in my mind, done the best work in helping us understand the word. In his *Old Testament Theology*, he writes:

> There is absolutely no concept in the Old Testament with so central a significance for all the relationships of human life as that of [righteousness]. It is the standard not only for man's relationship to God, but also for his relationships to his fellows, reaching right down to the most petty wranglings— indeed, it is even the standard for man's relationship to the animals and to his natural environment.[2]

Notice the repetition of the word "relationship"? That is because relationship is what righteousness is all about. Dr. von Rad argues that righteousness is not about living up to legal principles and standards. Rather, righteousness is all about living in faithfulness to the terms of relationship. Righteousness is

---

2 Gerhard von Rad, *Old Testament Theology: Volume 1: The Theology of Israel's Historical Traditions*, trans. D.M.G. Stalker (New York: Harper & Row, 1962), 370.

about living up to the particular claims any given relationship lays upon us.[3]

A spouse is righteous who lives up to the terms of the marriage covenant. A citizen is righteous who lives up to the expectation of the civil order. "Righteous" therefore simply means "in-right-relationship" or "right-relatedness." "Blessed are those who hunger and thirst for right-relationships, for right-relatedness." The term "righteousness" is found everywhere in the Biblical Story because the Biblical Story is all about right-relationship!

It is in this light that we are to understand God's gift of the Ten Commandments. The apostle Paul, the apostle of grace, calls God's commandments "the law of righteousness" (Romans 9:31), for the commandments are all about relationship. The Ten Commandments are not an arbitrary code of ethics God imposes on us. No, the Ten Commandments are an exposition of the right-relatedness that flows from a right-relationship with the Living God.

What is the first line of the Law? Most people answer, "You shall have no other gods before me." But that is not the first line. The first line is "I am Yahweh your God, who brought you out of the land of Egypt, out of the house of slavery" (Exodus 20:2). The Law begins with a declaration of relationship: "I am your God." It is the language of the Covenant God saying, "Before you hear anything else from Me, hear that I have already established a relationship with you. I am your God, you are My people."

---

3 See Ibid., 371-374.

In the Ten Commandments, which follow the first lines of the Law, God is simply unfolding the nature of the divinely initiated right-relatedness. It is as though God is saying, "Look, I am your God and you are My people. Now that that is settled, here is what our right-relatedness is going to look like: You will have no gods between us. No one or nothing will take the place I have in your life. You will live by a new rhythm of time, by My sabbatical rhythm: six days of work, one day of rest. You will honor father and mother. You will not commit adultery. You will not covet." The Law is not a list of dos and don'ts that we must obey in order to enter into relationship with God; the Law is simply a picture of the right-relatedness brought into being by God's grace.

You can see then that disobedience is so grievous not because a code of ethics has been violated, but because a relationship has not been taken seriously.

"Blessed are those who hunger and thirst for right-relationship, for they and only they shall be satisfied."

Many scholars argue that the theological center of the Sermon on the Mount, which the Beatitudes introduce, is Matthew 5:20, where Jesus says, "For I say to you, unless your righteousness surpasses that of the scribes and Pharisees, you will not enter the kingdom of heaven." Yikes! Surpasses? My righteousness must surpass the righteousness of the teachers of the Law and those who thought of themselves as spiritual giants?

Surpass? How in heaven's name are those grabbed by the gospel to live a "surpassing righteousness"? By realizing that the scribes and the Pharisees had missed the point. They thought of righteousness in terms of external conformity to the letter of the Law. But as Jesus shows us, one can obey the letter of the Law and not at all be faithful to the relationship being protected by the Law (5:21-48).

Thus a woman could say to herself, "I am righteous towards my neighbor as long as I do not cause his blood to flow," ignoring the issues of anger and words of insult, which also damage relationships. A man could say to himself, "I am righteous towards that woman as long as I do not sleep with her," ignoring the issue of lustful fantasies whereby he is using her for his own ends, which also damages relationship.

For Jesus, the righteousness of the kingdom goes beyond legality. Just because an action is legal does not make it righteous. Just because an attitude is culturally acceptable does not make it righteous. Righteous means being faithful to relationship, which means dealing with others on more fundamental levels of honesty and justice and mercy and servanthood. It is to these more basic levels that Jesus calls us.

"Righteousness" is all about relational integrity and wholeness, a relational integrity and wholeness that encompass the totality of life. "Blessed are those who crave relational wholeness."

OUR FOUR BASIC RELATIONSHIPS

Scripture teaches us that we were created for four basic relationships, relationships that are constitutive of our existence in the image of God. These four relationships are most clearly laid before us in the opening chapters of the Bible, in Genesis 1-2.

First, we were made for a relationship with the earth (Genesis 2:7). We are physical, material, ecological creatures. The Hebrew word for human is *adam*; the Hebrew word for earth is *adamah*. Our welfare is tied up with the welfare of the earth.

Second, we were made for a relationship with other human beings (Genesis 2:18, 22). We are social creatures. None of us is whole in isolation; we were created for community. The Hebrew word for man is *ish*; the Hebrew word for woman is *ishah*. We were made for fellowship with others.

Third, we were made for a relationship with the self (Genesis 2:25). We are psychological creatures. We were originally made to embrace ourselves as beloved without any guilt or shame.

And fourth, and most fundamentally, we were made for a relationship with the Living God. This relationship holds all the other relationships together. We are spiritual creatures, designed for trusting, obeying, enjoying, loving, and experiencing God's own delight in being God to us. We were made for a holistic relationship:

A right-relatedness with the created environment;

A right-relatedness with other humans;

A right-relatedness with our inner selves;

And a right-relatedness with the Holy One.

HUNGER AND THIRST

We cannot read the Biblical Story without catching God's own hunger and thirst for this complete right-relatedness. This means that we cannot read the whole story without encountering grief—God's grief. For the created order is now marked by so much unrighteousness: alienation, estrangement, manipulation, fear, hatred, violence, and death. This is all because we have turned our backs on the relationship with the Creator, which causes all the other relationships to unravel.

"Blessed, blessed, blessed are those who, like God, hunger and thirst for a full-ordered righteousness."

Jesus uses very intense verbs to describe this craving. William Barclay observes:

> The hunger which this beatitude describes is no genteel hunger which could be satisfied with a mid-morning snack; the thirst of which it speaks is no thirst which could be slaked with a cup of coffee or an iced drink. It is the hunger of the man who is starving for food; and the thirst of the man who will die unless he drinks.[4]

Jesus is not blessing those who are mildly dissatisfied with themselves and the world. He is blessing those who, as Dale Bruner puts it, "do not believe they can live unless they find righteousness."[5] "Blessed is the person who longs for righteousness as though his or her life depended on it."[6]

---

4 Barclay, *The Gospel of Matthew: Volume 1*, 99-100.
5 Bruner, *The Christbook*, 142.
6 Donald W. McCullough, *Finding Happiness in the Most Unlikely Places*, 79.

Why this intensity? Why does this massive craving emerge in the souls of those grabbed by Jesus and His gospel?

Because the gospel is all about righteousness! The kingdom of God that is breaking into the world in Jesus is all about right-relatedness. The gospel is the good news that the Righteous God, the God of all right-relationship, has not given up! The Creator's intense passion that all of creation enjoy right-relatedness will not be denied. In Jesus, God enters our unrighteous world and begins to reconstruct our four-fold relational existence.

The apostle Paul tells the believers living in Rome, "I am not ashamed of the gospel" (Romans 1:16). "Why?" we ask. "Because," Paul answers, "in the gospel the righteousness of God breaks through." The gospel of God is all about God "righteous-ing" all our unchecked relationships. In Jesus, God is repairing all our relationships: with God, with the self, with other humans, and with the earth. The resurrection of Jesus is God's guarantee that God is going to see the job through to completion.

And that is why Jesus blesses those who crave righteousness: they are craving what the Living God craves. Congratulations! You are alive with the Divine appetite! You are alive in the Passion of God Himself! In sync are those who crave right-relationship with the earth. In sync are those who crave right-relationship with others, who seek reconciliation between individuals, groups, and nations as though their lives depended on it, who starve for authentic community where people relate beyond the masses, who starve for justice in law courts, integrity in business, and fidelity in marriage.

"They shall be satisfied," says Jesus. Only they shall be satisfied. No other satisfaction is promised.

When will they be satisfied?

On that day when the kingdom of God breaks through all the way. On that day when the reconstruction job is finally completed.

But because Jesus has already come and is present, because the kingdom is already near, our hunger and thirst can be met to a large degree even today, because every day Jesus offers us Himself.

Every day Jesus offers us Himself as the source and embodiment of all right-relatedness. As He said to a very thirsty woman by a well in Samaria, so He says to us: "Ask of Me, and I will give you living water" (see John 4:10). As He said to those who had their fill of religion but were bone dry, so He says to us: "If anyone is thirsty, let him come to Me and drink... from his innermost being will flow rivers of living water" (John 7:37-38).

We cannot come just once. For when we come, He awakens even deeper longings for even more of Him. The bread of life satisfies, and yet any taste makes us hunger for more! The living water quenches, and yet every sip makes us thirst for more! George MacDonald said, "In things spiritual, increasing desire is the sign that satisfaction is drawing nearer."[7] Or, as philosopher Peter Kreeft puts it: "Dissatisfaction is the second best thing there is, because it dissolves the glue that entraps us to false satisfactions, and drives us to God, the only true satisfaction."[8]

Do you see where we have come? It turns out that the hunger and thirst for righteousness is hunger and thirst for Righteousness Himself! Saint Augustine was right: All our longings are, in the final analysis, longings for God.[9] So much so that Bruce Marshall can say that "the young man who rings the bell at the brothel is unconsciously looking for God."[10] He may not realize it, but his looking for a woman is symptomatic of his looking for God.

"Blessed are those who are going to die unless they find God."

---

7 George MacDonald, *The Hope of the Gospel* (London: Ward, Lock, Bowden and Co., 1892), 129.

8 Kreeft, *For Heaven's Sake*, 160.

9 Augustine famously said "you [God] have made us for yourself, and our heart is restless until it rests in you" (*Confessions*, trans. Henry Chadwick (Oxford: Oxford University Press, 1991), 3 (I.i.)). C.S. Lewis further developed this thinking—see Peter Kreeft, "C.S. Lewis's Argument from Desire" in *G.K. Chesterton and C.S. Lewis: The Riddle of Joy*, ed. Michael H. Macdonald and Andrew A. Tadie (Grand Rapids: William B. Eerdmans, 1989), 249-272.

10 Bruce Marshall, *The World, The Flesh, and Father Smith* (Boston: Houghton Mifflin, 1945), 108. The quote is regularly misattributed to G.K. Chesterton.

6

BEATITUDE FIVE
MERCY!

MATTHEW 5:7

"Blessed are the merciful, for they shall receive mercy." From my perspective, this fifth Beatitude is both the least paradoxical and the most paradoxical of all the eight.

I hear the fifth Beatitude and my heart says "of course!" Of course the Savior of the world congratulates mercy. I hear the other Beatitudes and say "really?" Blessed are the poor in spirit? Those who mourn? The meek? The persecuted? Really? But when I hear Jesus declare, "Right-on are the merciful," I say, "Yes, this makes sense." It is the least paradoxical of all the Beatitudes.

But then when Jesus begins to unfold the nature of mercy, I soon begin to think, "Oh, my goodness! This quality feels even more upside down than the others!" To practice mercy is to practice a profoundly paradoxical way of being.

Of all the character traits Jesus blesses in His Beatitudes, being merciful is the most measurable. More than the others, this one is "worn on the sleeve," so to speak. As William

Barclay puts it, "this mercy lodges in the heart, but expresses itself in the hand."[1]

"Blessed are the merciful, for they shall receive mercy."

As I have done with the other Beatitudes, I want to ask a number of questions of the fifth Beatitude.

Question one: Why is being merciful a mark of those who have been grabbed by Jesus and His good news? Why is being merciful a symptom of the time being fulfilled and the kingdom of God coming near?

Question two: What is this mercy that Jesus blesses? Can we get some practical handles on this kingdom quality?

Question three: What does Jesus mean by "shall be shown mercy," "shall obtain mercy"? Is Jesus saying that we merit mercy by being merciful? I think Jesus is clearly saying that mercy begets mercy; that is, the more we experience mercy the more we extend mercy. But is Jesus also saying that unless we extend mercy to others we will not receive mercy from God? In this series of studies, I have noted that the pronoun "theirs/they" is in the emphatic position: it comes at the beginning of the clause to say, "theirs and only

---

1 William Barclay, *The Beatitudes and the Lord's Prayer for Everyman* (New York: Harper & Row, 1963), 72.

theirs," "they and only they." Is Jesus saying that only the merciful are shown mercy? Does He mean that if I withhold mercy from others, God will withhold mercy from me? Oh, mercy!

WHY MERCY IS A MARK OF THE KINGDOM

Why is being "merciful" a character trait of those grabbed by Jesus and His gospel? For a number of reasons. First, Jesus, who announces the gospel, is Himself merciful. The exact word Jesus uses in the fifth Beatitude [*eleemones*] is used in only one other place in the New Testament, in the book of Hebrews. After affirming the real and full humanity of Jesus the Son of God, the author writes: "Therefore, He had to be made like His brethren in all things, so that He might become a merciful and faithful high priest" (Hebrews 2:17). Jesus *is* mercy.

What did the people of Palestine experience when they first met Jesus of Nazareth? Why were they drawn to Him? Unlike them, He was holy. Yet they flocked to be His. Why? Because, unexpectedly, the Holy One was merciful. Thus the cry, heard over and over again in the gospels: "Lord, have mercy on me." The cry was drawn out of their hearts by the realization, often unconscious, that here was Mercy Himself. Anyone who encounters Jesus, enters into relationship with Him, and shares His life will soon begin to take on something of His mercy.

Furthermore, not only is He merciful, but mercy is one of His greatest concerns; it is at the top of His agenda. The Pharisees, the self-righteous ones, criticized Jesus for eating with "tax-collectors and sinners." Jesus responded, "It is not those who are healthy who need a physician, but those who are sick. But go and learn what this means: 'I desire compassion [mercy], and not sacrifice,' for I did not come to call the righteous, but sinners" (Matthew 9:12-13). The Pharisees, the rule-keepers, the rule-enforcers, criticized Jesus for picking grain on the Sabbath. Jesus responded, "If you had known what this means, 'I desire compassion [mercy], and not a sacrifice,' you would not have condemned the innocent" (Matthew 12:7). During Holy Week, Jesus spoke a series of "woes" to the religious establishment. "Woe to you, scribes and Pharisees, hypocrites! [Note that this shows that mercy is not afraid to speak hard truth.] For you tithe mint and dill and cummin, and have neglected the weightier provisions of the law: justice and mercy and faithfulness" (Matthew 23:23).

Hang around Jesus long enough, and you cannot but begin to take on His bent toward mercy.

The third reason mercy is a mark of those grabbed by the gospel is that the kingdom that is breaking into history in Jesus is a kingdom of mercy. This is why the good news is "good" news. God's new world order has come near, and it is a new order of mercy.

At a dinner party, one of the Pharisees said to Jesus, "Blessed is everyone who will eat bread in the kingdom of God" (Luke 14:15). Luke then tells us that tax-collectors and sinners started coming to Jesus to listen to Him, and Jesus welcomed them and shared bread with them. The Pharisees and scribes were horrified and began to grumble, saying, "This man receives sinners and eats with them" (Luke 15:2). They said this in disgust and anger. Jesus then told His most beloved parable, the one about the father and his two sons. The younger son blows it—he is afraid to approach the father, but out of desperation risks returning home. Jesus says, "while he [the son] was still a long way off, his father saw him and felt compassion for him, and ran and embraced him and kissed him" (Luke 15:20).

Jesus is showing us that the God of the kingdom of God is the Father of mercy. If that kingdom is breaking into our lives, we cannot help becoming all caught up in mercy.

THE NATURE OF MERCY

What is this mercy that Jesus embodies and blesses?

As I hear Jesus, He comes at it both negatively and positively. Negatively: mercy is not giving someone what they deserve. Positively: mercy is giving someone what they do not deserve.

Negatively, mercy is not giving what is deserved. This is the way the word is used in a court of law. The plaintiff appeals to the judge, "Have mercy on me—do not give me what I deserve." And the gospel according to Jesus is just that: God, the Judge, not giving us what we deserve. Amazing mercy, how sweet the sound!

This is all the more amazing when we remember that the essential character of the Living God demands that our sin be punished; indeed, that sin be annihilated. God is holy. Holiness, by its very nature, cannot stand the presence of unholy sin. Holiness, by its very nature, naturally recoils from all that is not holy. God's very being, by nature, seeks to consume sin in the fire of purity. It would be perfectly just for God the Judge to wipe us out.

But what has God the Holy One done? At the cross, the Holy One expressed holy indignation against sin, but expressed it against Himself! In Jesus, the Holy One became one of us. But not only one of us, He became *us*. He not only became human; He became the Representative Human. Pontius Pilate posted over the head of Jesus on the cross the sign, "Here is the King of the Jews." But as many scholars have suggested, had the Holy God written the sign it would have read, "Here is the whole sinful human race." As the apostle Paul so daringly puts it, God "made Him who knew no sin to be sin on our behalf" (2 Corinthians 5:21).

Mercy! God Himself took upon Himself our sin. And then God Himself took upon Himself the awful judgment we deserve. The Holy God does not give me what I deserve. He does not give you what you deserve. He gives Himself what we deserve!

In light of what God did on the cross, you can see that being merciful does not mean ignoring the gravity of sin. It does not mean saying, "Oh, it does not matter." It does matter! The cross says it matters terribly. Being merciful simply means not giving a person what they justly deserve.

And positively, mercy extends undeserved blessing. New Testament scholar Robert Guelich suggests that in the Bible this positive understanding of mercy "points in two directions."[2] Mercy is "kindness shown one in need" (Psalm 86:15-16, Isaiah 30:18, Ezekiel 39:25, Mark 10:47).[3] Thus the phrase "acts of mercy" (Matthew 6:2-4). Mercy is also "pardon accorded one in the wrong" (Exodus 34:6-7, Isaiah 55:7, Matthew 18:32-34).[4] Mercy is extending kindness to the helpless and pardon to the guilty.

And the One who speaks this Beatitude exemplifies both of these positive directions of mercy. Jesus extends kindness to us who are in great need, who are so utterly helpless. Jesus extends pardon to us who are in the wrong, who owe a debt we can never pay. We were drowning, and Jesus dove into the water to rescue us. We were crushed beneath a horrible debt, and Jesus canceled it. Mercy!

Let us dig deeper.

Mercy is kindness to those in need. In Jesus' parable of the Good Samaritan (found in Luke 10:25-37), He develops this idea further. Jesus tells the story of a man who traveled the treacherous road that winds down from Jerusalem to Jericho in the desert. I have walked on this road, with its desolate, dangerous twists and turns. Along the way some robbers overtook the man, stripped him, and left him half-dead. A certain priest happened by, but when he saw the man lying on the side of the road, he did nothing to help. Then a certain Levite happened by, but when he saw the man on the road, he too did nothing

---

2 Guelich, The Sermon on the Mount, 88.
3 Ibid.
4 Ibid.

to help. But, says Jesus, a certain Samaritan happened by, and, says Jesus, "he felt compassion" (Luke 10:33). He felt mercy. The Samaritan poured oil and wine on the man's wounds and wrapped them in bandages. The Samaritan then put the man on his own beast, brought him to an inn and "took care of him," says Jesus. Because he still had other matters to which he needed to attend, the next morning he gave the innkeeper the equivalent of two days' wages, asking the innkeeper to continue the care, and promising to return and pay any further costs. Mercy is kindness to those in need.

Now, note that the Samaritan did not need to know why the man was in need. He extended kindness regardless of how the man got himself into that mess. We assume that the beaten man was an innocent victim, but maybe he was not. Maybe he had offended someone and the beating was an act of revenge. Or, maybe he had been involved in some illegal transaction, and not fulfilled his part of the bargain, and was being "liquidated." Or maybe he had bad-mouthed his assailants, taunting them into their brutal act. The Good Samaritan, as he has come to be called, did not need to know why the man was suffering. It did not matter. It would not have changed his actions. Mercy extends kindness to the needy regardless of the reason for the need.

How many of us withhold kindness when we discover that the one in need caused his or her own problem? Yes, some people are poor because they gambled away their income. Yes, some are on the streets because they lack initiative. The merciful simply see the need and look for ways to bring help. Some who have HIV contracted it innocently, as children or through tainted blood transfusions. Others who have HIV are not "innocent victims." They could have protected themselves by not using dirty needles to get a drug fix, or by not messing with God's design for human sexuality. "So?" ask the merciful. The merciful simply see the need and seek ways to bring help.

Note also that the Good Samaritan *risked* in order to extend kindness. Mercy always involves risk. Mercy may involve risking loss of time, loss of money, loss of health, or loss of reputation. The priest in Jesus' parable knew he would risk losing ritual purity to get involved. The Levite knew he would risk becoming a target for the bandits. The Samaritan pushed through his fears. He knew he could have been beaten himself, for in that culture, had the beaten man's friends come around the bend and seen the Samaritan near the victim, they would—without asking—have assumed the Samaritan had done the beating, and they would have retaliated. Mercy risks for the sake of the other.

Is not the Good Samaritan a picture of Jesus? He risks everything to extend kindness to us. He especially risks the Divine reputation. He loses face with the religious people of the day. "This man receives sinners and eats with them" (Luke 15:2) was meant as a put-down—a slam on Jesus. So be it. Mercy does not worry about the loss of name.

Mercy is kindness toward those in need.

Mercy is also pardon for those in debt. Jesus develops for us this aspect of mercy in the parable of the Unmerciful Slave (Matthew 18:21-35). Jesus' disciple Peter asks: "How often shall my brother sin against me and I forgive him? Up to seven times?" (18:21). Peter thinks he is being quite magnanimous—up to seven times! Jesus responds, "I do not say to you, up to seven times, but up to seventy times seven" (18:22). Up to 490 times!

Then Jesus tells the story of a king who wanted to settle accounts with his slaves. A slave who owes the king ten thousand talents—more than a day laborer could make in 200,000 years!—begs for mercy: "Have patience with me, and I will repay you everything."[5] Right! And, Jesus says, the lord "felt compassion," felt mercy, and released the slave, cancelling all the debt. This unthinkably large sum of money was just erased from the ledger. The forgiven slave then meets up with a fellow slave who owes him about four months' wages, and the forgiven slave demands payment.[6] The slave owing the smaller amount appeals for mercy: "Have patience with me, and I will repay you." But the forgiven slave will not listen to the cry, and turns the fellow slave in to prison until the debt can be paid. When all the other slaves of the king witness this, they are "deeply grieved" and report to their lord all that has happened. The lord summons the unforgiving-forgiven-slave and says, "I forgave you all that debt because you pleaded with me. Should you not also have had mercy on your fellow slave, in the same way that I had mercy on you?" (Matthew 18:32-33). And the lord puts the unmerciful slave in prison. And Jesus ends the story: "My heavenly Father will also do the same to you, if each

5 The text says that the debt was 10,000 talents. A talent was approximately what a day laborer would make in 20 years of work.
6 The Greek is a hundred denarii, with a denarius being a day's wage for a day laborer.

of you does not forgive his brother from your heart" (18:35). Mercy cancels debts.

Is not the lord in the parable a picture of our Lord, to whom we owe a horrendous debt? Dale Bruner, in his commentary on the parable, points out that the rabbis of Jesus' day taught that

> every sin created a certain deposit of debt before God, the accumulation of which formed a kind of separating wall between the person and God. On the other hand every righteous deed contributed to the believer's accumulation of assets before God and so created a kind of bridge. Sins were demerits that separated; righteous deeds were merits that connected. The corporate name for those separate demerits was "debts."[7]

Jesus uses that very word in His parable. And with it, He announces His gospel. The Lord of lords cancels debts! When we come before Him and confess that we owe a huge debt, and confess that we can never pay it, He cancels it! Mercy!

This is what Jesus gives us the freedom to pray in the Lord's Prayer. "Our Father in heaven... forgive us our debts as we forgive our debtors." Father—cancel our debts. And He does! The Father pardons us; He removes the debts and the separating wall the debts create. And He does so at a horrendous price: the price of the incarnation and crucifixion. As an anonymous Chinese pastor is reported to have said, "He came

---

7 Bruner, *The Christbook*, 251.

to pay a debt He did not owe because we owed a debt we could not pay."[8]

So, what is this mercy Jesus embodies and blesses? His mercy towards us: not giving us what we justly deserve, and giving us what we do not deserve—kindness in our helplessness, pardon of our indebtedness.

DO ONLY THOSE WHO SHOW MERCY RECEIVE MERCY?

When Jesus says, "Blessed are the merciful, for they shall be shown mercy," is He saying that only those who are merciful toward others will receive mercy from God?

From everything Jesus says—especially in the first Beatitude—"Blessed are the poor in spirit"—we know that he is not saying that before God will extend mercy to us, we must first extend mercy to others. The gospel declares that God's mercy comes first; God's mercy breaks in, enabling us to know and express mercy.

Then is Jesus saying that if we withhold mercy from others, God will withhold mercy from us? After giving us the Lord's Prayer, Jesus says, "For if you forgive others for their transgressions, your heavenly Father will also forgive you. But if you do not forgive others, then your Father will not forgive your transgressions" (Matthew 6:14-15). Is Jesus saying that if we do not cancel the debts of others, God will not cancel our debts?

I have wrestled with this for years. At this point in the journey, I think Jesus is saying that if we are *asking* God for mercy *while refusing* mercy for someone else, we are *not*—in

---

8 This also became the chorus of a popular 1970s worship song.

that moment—actually asking God for mercy. Oh, we are using the words: "Father, have mercy on me, cancel my debts." But we are *not, in that moment, actually living in the reality of the words.* In that moment—when I am refusing mercy for another, I am not grasping what I am asking for myself. To refuse to pardon another is to refuse to cancel the other's debts. How can I genuinely be asking God to cancel any debt while refusing to cancel another's debt? In that moment, when I am refusing to give another person mercy, I am implicitly saying that he or she must first pay his or her debt. If I go into God's presence with that frame of mind, it means that in spite of my words, I either think I have paid my debt, or think I can pay it. In either case, it means that in that moment, I am not seeking mercy. I am seeking to justify myself before God. If I ask for mercy from God but am not willing to extend it to another, I am not really asking for mercy. I have lost touch with who I am before God.

This is where the interrelatedness of the eight Beatitudes comes into play. The merciful whom Jesus blesses are also poor in spirit; they know their own spiritual poverty and need for mercy. The merciful whom Jesus blesses are also those who mourn; they know their own brokenness and twistedness and grieve over their own sin. The merciful whom Jesus blesses are also meek; they know they have no other hope in life but the mercy of God. The merciful whom Jesus blesses are also those who hunger and thirst for right-relatedness; they know they have not arrived, but crave to be all God wants them to be.

You can see then that it is in those moments when we cannot extend mercy—and some of those moments are very painful because we have been so deeply hurt or violated—that we are most in need of mercy. And here is the good news, the gospel: When in that moment we cry out "Lord have mercy," He does. He comes near, so very near. Mercy Himself comes near, and then empowers us to do for others what He has done for us.

Blessed, in sync with the heart of the Father, with the heart of the Holy God, are those who practice mercy; who do not give those who sin against them what those who sin against them deserve, but who give those who sin against them what they do not deserve—kindness and pardon—for they shall be shown mercy upon mercy upon mercy.

Mercy!

7

BEATITUDE SIX
SEE GOD? REALLY?

MATTHEW 5:8

"Blessed are the pure in heart, for they shall see God."

For me, this is the most arresting of all the Beatitudes. It is also my favorite. The sixth Beatitude is the one I cling to the most. Of all the qualities Jesus blesses, the one I most want to have is purity of heart. And of all the blessings Jesus promises, to "see God" is the one I most desire.

As far as I am concerned, this is the greatest promise Jesus ever made—"see God." To be promised the kingdom of heaven, to be promised comfort in sorrow, to be promised satisfaction of our hunger and thirst for right-relatedness, to be promised mercy for mercy, to be promised the name "son of God" or "daughter of God," or to be promised the earth, are all wonderful enough. But to be promised "they shall see God"? It is more than wonderful. You lucky bums indeed! Everything else pales in its light. Everything else comes into focus in its light. "They shall see God."

I want to ask just one question of the Beatitude (although the question will raise a host of others!). And I want to ask the same question of both clauses of the Beatitude—of the "pure in heart" clause and of the "see God" clause. The question is: "Is it really possible?" Is it really possible to be "pure in heart"? Is it really possible to "see God"?

SEEING GOD

Let us work with the "see God" clause first.

"See"—in what sense? I am not sure; no one is sure. Jesus' promise brings us into a place of great mystery. How is Jesus using the verb "see"? Literally? Figuratively? Metaphorically? Is He referring to a seeing with the so-called "eye of faith"? As we sing, "Open the eyes of my heart, Lord. I want to see you"?[1]

Or, is Jesus promising the pure in heart that they will somehow "recognize" that there is a God, that this God is good, that this God is for them, that this God is present to them, that this God has come down in Jesus, and dwells with them and in them by the Holy Spirit? Is Jesus speaking of a kind of mental-emotional "cognition"?

Or, is Jesus saying that the pure in heart will see God in the same way they see other dimensions of reality? That they will see God in the same way they see people and trees and mountains and buildings?

If that is what He means, then the question becomes "What do they see?" Is there some "thing" to be seen? On the one hand, there is what the apostle Paul writes in his first letter to his colleague Timothy. In the opening chapter, Paul speaks

---

1 Paul Baloche, "Open the Eyes of My Heart," Integrity's Hosanna! Music, 1997.

of God as "eternal, immortal, invisible" (1 Timothy 1:17). In the closing chapter, Paul speaks of God "who alone possesses immortality and dwells in unapproachable light, whom no man has seen or can see" (1 Timothy 6:16).

Yet on the other hand, there are all those puzzling, mysterious texts scattered throughout the whole of the Biblical Story. I think of the story of the patriarch Jacob, the story in which he wrestles with "a man" all night long (Genesis 32:22-32). As the story unfolds, Jacob concludes that he had actually been wrestling with God. The text then says, "So Jacob named the place Peniel [i.e., the face of God] for he said, 'I have seen God face to face, yet my life has been preserved'" (Genesis 32:30).

I think of the story of Moses, the great leader of the Exodus, the story in which he is confronted by his sister and brother but vindicated by God. God says to Moses' sister and brother: "Hear now My words: If there is a prophet among you, I, the Lord, shall make Myself known to him in a vision. I shall speak with him in a dream. Not so, with my servant Moses, he is faithful in all My household; with him I speak mouth to mouth, even openly, and not in dark sayings, and he beholds the form of the Lord" (Numbers 12:6-8).

Moses beholds the form of Yahweh, the Living God? Is there a form to behold? Is this merely metaphorical language? What did Moses see?

There are evenings when, after finishing whatever tasks I can, I sit in a chair or lie on the bed and let my brain wander into the vast expanses of outer space. Within seconds, I am way beyond Mars and Jupiter and Neptune, way beyond the nearest black hole. I let myself be awed by the sheer magnitude of it all. And then, realizing that the Living God is so much bigger than even this, and realizing that it is all held together moment by moment by His word, I allow the question to surface, if only for a moment, "What is God?" Not "who" but "what"? What are You, Lord? What is this Reality that transcends it all and yet graciously chooses to meet with us? "They shall see God." What shall they see?

Another question quickly follows. Can we see and live? Can human beings handle seeing whatever is "see-able" of God? Again I think of the story of Moses, the one in which he cries out to God, "show me Your glory" (Exodus 33:18). Show me Your kabod, your weightiness, show me that which makes you be God! My heart echoes Moses' prayer—"show me Your glory!"

God responds, "I Myself will make all My goodness pass before you, and will proclaim the Name of Yahweh before you; and I will be gracious to whom I will be gracious, and will show compassion on whom I will show compassion.... You cannot see My face, for no man can see me and live" (Exodus 33:19-20). God then tells Moses to hide in the cleft of a rock, and says "I will cover you with My hand until I have passed by. Then I will take My hand away and you shall see My back, but My face shall not be seen" (Exodus 33:22-23). "No human may see Me and live."

Yet Jesus says, "Blessed are the pure in heart, for they shall see." Is Jesus thereby implying that Moses was not pure in heart? Is Jesus saying that the "no human" in the phrase "no human may see Me and live" is an impure human, but that a pure human can see and live? Is this the point of what is revealed to the apostle John on the island of Patmos?

> Then I saw a new heaven and a new earth; for the first heaven and the first earth passed away… And I heard a loud voice from the throne, saying, "Behold, the tabernacle of God is among men, and He will dwell among them… There will no longer be any curse; and the throne of God and of the Lamb will be in it, and His bond-servants will serve Him; they will see His face" (Revelation 21:1, 3; 22:3-4).

In the new creation, has something happened to human beings that enable them to behold the dazzling beauty and raw glory and live?

What is clear is what is developed for us in the Gospel according to John. John begins his story of Jesus on this note: "No one has seen God at any time; the only begotten God [referring to Jesus] who is in the bosom of the Father, He has explained Him"—He has made God known (John 1:18). As we read on, we then hear Jesus say things like, "He who believes in Me, does not believe in Me but in Him who sent Me. He who sees Me sees the One who sent Me" (John 12:44-45). One of Jesus' disciples, Philip, says to Jesus, "Show us the Father, and it is enough for us." Jesus responds, "Have I been so long with you, and yet you have not come to know Me, Philip? He who has seen Me has seen the Father" (John 14:8-9). The unseen has become see-able in Jesus.

Thus, the apostle Paul can make the great claim that Jesus Christ is "the image [the visible expression] of the invisible God" (Colossians 1:15). In his second letter to the Corinthians, Paul writes: "God, who said, 'Light shall shine out of darkness,' is the One who has shone in our hearts to give us the Light of the knowledge of the glory of God in the face of Christ" (2 Corinthians 4:6). In Jesus of Nazareth, infinitude is focused. In Jesus, the Living God takes on a face, for in Jesus, the face of the Living God is made manifest, enabling the impure to see and live.

This affirmation raises yet another question, a practical question. Where is the face of Jesus now, so that we may behold in His face the face of the Infinite?

Apparently it is not very far away. For what did He tell His disciples who longed for a clearer vision? Pointing to a group of children, He said, "Whoever receives one child like this in My name receives Me; and whoever receives Me does not receive Me, but Him who sent Me" (Mark 9:37). Jesus is saying that somehow we see His face in the face of the child who cries out for attention. In His parable of the sheep and the goats, Jesus speaks of being hungry and us feeding Him, of being a stranger and us welcoming Him, of being sick and us nursing Him. Then Jesus has us respond:

"Lord, when did we see You hungry, and feed You, or thirsty, and give You something to drink? And when did we see You a stranger, and invite You in, or naked and clothe You? When did we see You sick, or in prison, and come to You?" The King will answer and say to them, "Truly I say to you, to the extent you did it to one of these brothers of Mine, even to the least of them, you did it to Me" (Matthew 25:37-40).

Jesus is saying that somehow we see His face, and therefore the face of God, in the face of the world's marginalized. This is the secret to the joy Mother Teresa found in her work in Calcutta: She saw in the faces of discarded infants and discarded elders the face of the Lover of her soul. Is this what Jesus means by "see God"? That the pure in heart will recognize and embrace the Holy One in the midst of the ordinary?

Or is there more? Children, after all, are not Jesus. Yes, He comes to us in their coming to us, but they are not God. The hungry and strangers are not Jesus. Yes, He comes to us in their coming to us, but they are not God. So is there still another kind of seeing? And what do the pure in heart "see" when Jesus fulfills His promise?

I do not know. But whatever Jesus is promising, I want it. Whatever is involved in "seeing God," I want it. What is clear is that what we will see when we 'see God' is more beautiful than anything He has made. The beauty of His handiwork cannot compare with Beauty Himself!

BEING PURE IN HEART

Let us now work with the "pure in heart" clause. The human heart "sees" what it has the capacity to see. So what does Jesus mean by "pure in heart?" And is it really possible to have it, to be it?

In the Bible, the word "heart" does not only refer to the organ that pumps our blood. "Heart" refers to the center of the human person, to the home or seat of human feeling, thinking, and willing. The word "pure" in Greek is katharos, from which we develop the English words "cathartic" and "catharsis." It means to be clean. It means "un-mixed, un-alloyed, unadulterated," as in pure gold or pure maple syrup. "Pure in heart," therefore, means unmixed at the center, un-alloyed at the center, unadulterated at the center. O Jesus, please make it so!

Again, here is where it is so important to remember that in the Beatitudes Jesus is not describing eight different kinds of people: one who is poor in spirit, another who is merciful, still another who is pure in heart. Rather, Jesus is describing eight qualities of the same person. The eight kingdom qualities are all interrelated. And the order in which Jesus presents them is no accident. I believe the order is intentional. Jesus does not begin with "pure in heart" because it needs to be heard and seen in light of the qualities that precede it.

Thus, the "pure in heart" Jesus blesses are also "poor in spirit." I should say, they are first and foremost poor in spirit: they know their own spiritual bankruptcy. This means that the "pure in heart" are not perfect and they know it! The "pure in heart" whom Jesus blesses are also "those who mourn." They grieve over their sin and the sin of the world. The "pure in heart" have not arrived and they know it! The "pure in heart" whom Jesus blesses are "meek." They know they cannot make it on their own. The "pure in heart" also hunger and thirst for righteousness, craving to be so, meaning that "pure in heart" does not mean "perfect"! The "pure in heart" are also merciful. Their own poverty of spirit, grief, and hunger and thirst create a tenderness toward, and sympathy for, their fellow humans. The "pure in heart" understand and feel the common human struggles and failures. This is crucial to grasp.

It is helpful to look at how the term "pure in heart" is used elsewhere in the Bible. Of particular help is the way it is used in the Psalms, and in particular, Psalm 24:

"Who may ascend into the hill of the Lord?
And who may stand in His holy place?
He who has clean hands and a pure heart,
who has not lifted up his soul to falsehood
and has not sworn deceitfully" (Psalm 24:3-4).

In this text, "purity of heart" is elaborated as "not lifting one's soul to falsehood" and "not swearing deceitfully." This suggests that "purity of heart" has to do with integrity. "Blessed are those who have integrity at the center." Blessed are those who know how easy it is to be deceived and to play games with reality. Blessed are those who crave truth: who seek truth, face truth, tell truth, and live truth. J.B. Phillips can therefore render the sixth Beatitude as "Blessed are the utterly sincere." John Stott elaborates: "Their whole life, public and private, is transparent before God and men."[2]

Again, the "pure in heart" are not perfect. It is just that they know they cannot hide anything from God. So, living

---

2 John R.W. Stott, *Christian Counter-Culture: The Message of the Sermon on the Mount* (Downers Grove: InterVarsity Press, 1978), 49.

in sync with the really real, they bring their thoughts, their emotions, their fears and dreams into the light of God's truth and grace.

One of the regular prayers of the "pure in heart" is given in the last verses of Psalm 139: "Search me, O God, and know my heart; try me and know my anxious thoughts; and see if there be any hurtful way in me" (vs 23-24). They pray this way because of the start of the Psalm: "O Lord, You have searched me and known me" (vs 1). There is no escaping God's presence and God's intimate knowing of us. The "pure in heart" know this and open up the whole of life to God's searching, cleansing, healing light.

"Congratulations," says Jesus, "for you shall see God!"

BECOMING PURE IN HEART

So how do we become "pure in heart"? How do we get this integrity and transparency at the center? By getting Jesus! By getting His gospel. Or, better yet, by Jesus getting us! By the gospel getting us!

"It is time," Jesus says. "It is time for the kingdom of heaven to come near." It is time for the world beyond to break into this world. It is time for heaven to come down to earth. It is time for God's new world order of truth to invade and transform every sector of life. As Matthew says just before recording the Beatitudes, quoting the prophet Isaiah: "The people who were sitting in darkness saw a great light" (Matthew 4:16; Isaiah 9:2).

It turns out that the light is a Person! Truth is a Person! When He gets a hold on us He begins to expose all the lies about ourselves and God. He awakens an abhorrence of hypocrisy and manipulation. He quickens a passion for integrity at the center of our being. You see? The "pure in heart" become what they become because Purity Himself has taken hold of their hearts. As philosopher Peter Kreeft put it, "We attain purity of heart not merely by the imitation of Christ but by the incorporation into Christ, the Christ who has perfect purity of heart."[3]

When the disciple Peter first met Jesus, he became aware of how impure he was. He fell down at Jesus' feet, crying out, "Go away from me, Lord, for I am a sinful man" (Luke 5:8). Steven Waldschmidt, an actor from Calgary, wrote a short play on that scene while he was a student at Regent College. In the play, he has Peter say to Jesus, "Go away from me, Jesus, because I will make you dirty." To which Steven has Jesus say, "No, Peter, you will not make me dirty; I will make you clean."

SAINT FRANCIS

A conversation St. Francis of Assisi had with a fellow monk takes us to the heart of the matter. As Francis and Brother Leo were walking together, Francis noticed that Leo was quite low, maybe even depressed. So Francis asked,

"Leo, do you know what it means to be pure of heart?"

---

3 Kreeft, *For Heaven's Sake*, 168-169.

"Of course. It means to have no sins, faults, or weaknesses to reproach myself for."

"Ah," said Francis, "now I understand why you're sad. We will always have something to reproach ourselves for."

"Right," said Leo. "That's why I despair of ever arriving at purity of heart."

"Leo, listen carefully to me. Don't be so preoccupied with the purity of your heart. Turn and look at Jesus. Admire Him. Rejoice that He is what He is—your Brother, your Friend, your Lord and Savior. That, little brother, is what it means to be pure of heart. And once you've turned to Jesus, don't turn back and look at yourself. Don't wonder where you stand with Him.

The sadness of not being perfect, the discovery that you really are sinful, is a feeling much too human, even borders on idolatry. Focus your vision outside yourself on the beauty, graciousness, and compassion of Jesus Christ. The pure of heart praise Him from sunrise to sundown. Even when they feel broken, feeble, distracted, insecure, and uncertain, they are able to release it into His peace. A heart like that is stripped and filled—stripped of self and filled with the fullness of God. It is enough that Jesus is Lord."

After a long pause, Leo said, "Still, Francis, the Lord demands our effort and fidelity."

"No doubt about that," replied Francis. "But holiness is not a personal achievement. It's an emptiness you discover in yourself. Instead of resenting it, you accept it and it becomes the free space where the Lord can create anew. To cry out, 'You alone are the Holy One, you alone are the Lord,' that is what it means to be pure of heart. And it doesn't come by your Herculean efforts and threadbare resolutions."

"Then how?" asked Leo.

"Simply hoard nothing of yourself; sweep the house clean. Sweep out even the attic, even the nagging, painful consciousness of your past. ...Renounce everything that is heavy, even the weight of your sins. See only the compassion, the infinite patience, and the tender love of Christ. Jesus is Lord. That suffices.... Even the desire for holiness is transformed into a pure and simple desire for Jesus."

Leo listened gravely as he walked along beside Francis. Step by step he felt his heart grow lighter as a profound peace flooded his soul.[4]

---

4 Manning, *Lion and Lamb*, 181-182.

"Blessed are the pure in heart, for they shall see God." See God? Yes!

Blessed are those who have left behind the preoccupation with how well they are doing and are simply captivated by Jesus of Nazareth. For they are seeing God!

Be Thou my Vision, O Lord of my heart;
Naught be all else to me, save that Thou art.
Thou my best Thought, by day or by night,
Waking or sleeping, Thy presence my light.

Be Thou my Wisdom, and Thou my true Word;
I ever with Thee and Thou with me, Lord;
Thou my great Father, I Thy true son;
Thou in me dwelling, and I with Thee one.

Be Thou my battle Shield, Sword for the fight;
Be Thou my Dignity, Thou my Delight;
Thou my soul's Shelter, Thou my high Tower:
Raise Thou me heavenward, O Power of my power.

Riches I heed not, nor man's empty praise,
Thou mine Inheritance, now and always:
Thou and Thou only, first in my heart,
High King of Heaven, my Treasure Thou art.

High King of Heaven, my victory won,
May I reach Heaven's joys, O bright Heaven's Sun!
Heart of my own heart, whatever befall,
Still be my Vision, O Ruler of all.[5]

---

5 "Be Thou My Vision," an ancient Irish hymn, translated by Mary E. Byrne, versified by Eleanor H. Hull.

8

BEATITUDE SEVEN
SHALOM-MAKERS

MATTHEW 5:9

"Blessed are the peacemakers."

This is probably the best known of all the Beatitudes. It has inspired more music then any of the others. It is found on more greeting cards and wall posters than any of the others. And rightly so. For in His seventh Beatitude, Jesus bestows incredible dignity on ordinary, broken human beings, as I trust this chapter will help you see and feel.

As I have noted throughout this series of studies, whenever we focus on just one Beatitude, we need to do so in relation to them all. We saw how important this is in the last chapter on the sixth Beatitude, "Blessed are the pure in heart, for they shall see God." "Purity of heart" has to be understood in light of poverty of spirit, and mourning, and gentleness, and hungering and thirsting for right-relatedness, and mercy. So too "peacemakers."

Here is where it is important to review the original context of the Beatitudes.

Jesus comes on the scene with what He calls "the gospel of God," God's good news for the world. The word translated "gospel," or good news, is the word euangelion, which came into English as a word we don't use much anymore, evangel. And from it, we have the related words "evangelize," meaning to "good-news-ize," and "evangelical," meaning "people with good news."

Jesus comes on the scene with God's evangel. The writers of the four Gospels are making a huge point in using this term, for the Roman emperors were using it for their edicts, their "throne speeches." They thought of themselves as "lords, saviors, and redeemers of the world," and their authoritative messages to the Empire were called euangelium.[1] "The idea was that what comes from the emperor is a saving message, that is not just a piece of news, but a change of the world for the better."[2]

So when the writers of the New Testament use the word euangelion relative to Jesus, they are saying to us: "What the emperors, who pretend to be gods, illegitimately claim, really occurs here... Here is the real Lord of the world—the Living God—who goes into action."[3]

So Jesus comes on the scene with God's evangel: "It is time... the kingdom of God has come near." Jesus begins to "evangelize"! Matthew tells us that Jesus begins healing all kinds of diseases, freeing people from all kinds of evil, forgiving sins, and welcoming broken people into His family (Matthew 4:23-25).

---

1 Joseph Ratzinger [Pope Benedict XVI], *Jesus of Nazareth: From the Baptism in the Jordan to the Transfiguration* (New York: Doubleday, 2007), 46.
2 Ibid., 47.
3 Ibid.

And then Jesus speaks His Beatitudes. The seventh: "Right-on, in sync with God's evangel, are the peacemakers, for they shall be called the children of God."

As I said, in this Beatitude, Jesus is bestowing incredible dignity on ordinary, broken people. "Makers." Peace-makers. Jesus is not here blessing "peace lovers," although He certainly could. Jesus is not here blessing "peace seekers," although He certainly could. Jesus is not here blessing "peace keepers," although He certainly could and does. Jesus is here congratulating "peace makers." Plain, old, imperfect folks… makers of peace?

THE NATURE OF PEACE

For most people, the word "peace" "usually refers either to an inner tranquility—peace of mind—or to an outward state – the absence of war."[4] The Biblical concept of peace certainly includes those ideas, but it goes far deeper and wider.

Behind the word used in the seventh Beatitude is the Hebrew word shalom. It means "soundness, well-being, wholeness." Shalom is life as God originally intended it to be: a well-rounded, holistic existence. Shalom involves harmony with the earth, harmony with other human beings, harmony with the inner self, and harmony with the Living God; shalom is ecological soundness, relational soundness, psychological soundness, and spiritual soundness. Shalom encompasses every dimension of life—the economic and political as well as the personal and religious.

From the perspective of the Bible, silencing the guns does not mean peace has come. By the Bible's standard, feeling good

4 Bruner, *The Christbook*, 149.

inside does not necessarily mean peace has come. Peace reigns when the causes of strife are healed. As Pope John Paul II said in a speech to the General Assembly of the United Nations, "Indeed, the fight against incipient wars cannot be carried out on a merely superficial level, by treating the symptoms. It must be done in a radical way, by attacking the causes."[5] He went on to talk about the two main threats to human rights: the unjust "distribution of material goods" and "injustice in the field of the spirit." I would add that peace can only come about by getting beyond human resistance to God and His Anointed One (Psalm 2).

The Biblical concept of peace involves so much more than inner tranquility and the absence of war! Shalom is a psycho-somatic, relational, economic, racial, and spiritual wholeness.

> "And the wolf will dwell with the lamb, and the leopard will lie down with the young goat… and the lion will eat straw like the ox" (Isaiah 11:6-7). That is shalom.

> "The wilderness and the desert will be glad… it will blossom profusely… the eyes of the blind will be opened and the ears of the deaf will be unstopped. Then the lame will leap like a deer, and the tongue of the mute will shout for joy" (Isaiah 35:1-2, 5-6). That is shalom.

---

5 The text of the speech can be found at www.vatican.va/holy_father/john_paul_ii/speeches/1979/ October/ documents/hf_jp-ii_spe_19791002_general-assembly-onu_en.html (accessed 27 February 2013).

"And they will hammer their swords into plowshares and their spears into pruning hooks" (Isaiah 2:4). That is shalom.

"So then you are no longer strangers and aliens, but you are fellow citizens with the saints, and are of God's household" (Ephesians 2:19). That is shalom.

"Having been built on the foundation of the apostles and prophets, Christ Jesus Himself being the corner stone, in whom the whole building, being fitted together is growing into a holy temple in the Lord" (Ephesians 2:20-21). That is shalom.

"And He will wipe away every tear from their eyes; and there will no longer be any death; there will no longer be any mourning, or crying, or pain" (Revelation 21:4). That is shalom; that is peace.

You see, then, why I say that in the seventh Beatitude Jesus bestows on us incredible dignity? We wounded human beings, makers of shalom? Lovers of shalom, of course. Seekers of shalom, of course. Keepers of shalom, maybe. But human beings, makers of shalom? Only the Living God can make shalom! Shalom is a Divine reality—a holistic soundness that only the holistic God can make. Yet Jesus calls those whom He calls to Himself "shalom-makers." This time, the rendering "you lucky bums" really captures the wonder.

When Jesus and His evangel get hold of an individual, a community, a city, or a nation, something happens. Ordinary, broken people become partners in a Divine work. Shalom makers. Oh, such dignity.

Again, in the Beatitudes, Jesus is not describing eight different kinds of kingdom people: one who is poor in spirit, another who mourns, another who is meek, another who is pure in heart. Rather, Jesus is describing eight different qualities of the same kingdom person. This means every person captured by Jesus and His gospel becomes poor in spirit; every good-news-ized person begins to hunger and thirst for right-relatedness; every "evangelized" person becomes merciful; and every "evangelical" is called to the shalom-making vocation. Every kingdom-ized, born again, Spirit-filled person—use whatever term you want—every disciple of Jesus is to be a shalom-maker. Not just a lover, or seeker, or keeper, but a maker!

PEACEMAKING AS A SIGN OF THE KINGDOM

Why is this a mark of those who have turned around and embraced Jesus and His good news of the kingdom? For two basic reasons.

First, Jesus the Evangelizer is the Man of Peace. He is Shalom Himself.

Isaiah 9, the great Christmas Eve text: "For a child will be born to us, a son will be given to us... and His name will be called Wonderful, Counselor, Mighty God, Eternal Father, Prince of Peace" (Isaiah 9:6).

Zechariah 9, the great Palm Sunday text: "Behold, your king is coming to you; He is just and endowed with salvation, humble, and mounted on a donkey… I will cut off the chariot from Ephraim and the horse from Jerusalem; and the bow of war will be cut off. And He will speak peace to the nations" (Zechariah 9:9-10).

The One who announces the gospel is the Prince of Peace, who speaks shalom into being. Those who enter into relationship with Him cannot but become, at the very least, shalom lovers and shalom seekers. As Dietrich Bonhoeffer puts it: when the disciples met Jesus of Nazareth, "they found their peace, for he is their peace."[6]

Second, peacemaking is a mark of those upon whom the kingdom has come because the kingdom is a kingdom of Peace. The new world order has come near, and it is an order of shalom. In Jesus, we see the soundness, the wholeness, the full-orbed well-being for which we were originally created. In Jesus' actions, we see shalom-in-the-making: restoration of harmony with the Living God, restoration of harmony with others, restoration of harmony with self, and restoration of harmony with the earth. When His new world order begins to break into our lives, we cannot help becoming, at the very least, shalom lovers and seekers. Jesus says we become more: we become shalom makers.

Well then, what does this peacemaking look like? What does it look like in the part of the world where you live? Jesus will unfold the answer in the sermon that follows the

---

6 Bonhoeffer, *The Cost of Discipleship*, 126.

Beatitudes, His Sermon on the Mount: the same answer He unfolds as He lives and dies in our world.

I do not know everything about the dignified vocation to which Jesus calls us. But I do know five things.

THE POSTURE FOR PEACEMAKING

First, I know the posture for peace. That is, I know the proper stance for receiving and experiencing peace. I know that shalom is a gift of God, a gift that can finally only be enjoyed in relationship with God. The peace of God is finally realized when God is allowed to be God.

On page after page the Bible puts its finger on the most basic cause of the unrest, anxiety, and strife that fills our world. It is that humanity has turned its back on our Maker. Believing that "God is dead" sadly leads, inexorably so, to violence and decay. Humanity refuses to live as a creature before the Creator. Human beings, even religious human beings, usurp the place and role of God and are, therefore, in a state of rebellion against God. Need I illustrate? The Theological Declaration of Barmen, written during the rise of Nazism, declares: "Just as Jesus Christ is God's comforting pronouncement of the forgiveness of all our sins, just so—and with the same earnestness—he is also God's vigorous announcement of his claim upon our whole life."[7] Resistance to God's mighty claim is at the root of all peace-less-ness. Until that resistance ends, shalom cannot be fully realized.

---

7 Rolf Ahlers, *The Barmen Theological Declaration of 1934: The Archaeology of a Confessional Text* (Lewiston, NY: Edwin Mellen Press, 1986), 40-41.

Is this not what the angels were getting at on Christmas Eve when they sang, "Glory to God in the highest and on earth peace" (Luke 2:14)? "Glory to God in the highest" is the infrastructure for "peace on earth." No glory to God, no peace. The shalom Jesus brings into the world is experienced when we bow the knee before the God who reigns, when we step off the throne of life and accept our place as creatures, as children, as followers. In a speech he gave at Stanford University, Vaclav Havel, the President of the Czech Republic, described the current world situation and ended by saying:

> Given its fatal incorrigibility, humanity probably will have to go through many more Rwandas and Chernobyls before it understands how unbelievably shortsighted a human being can be who has forgotten that he is not God.[8]

"Glory to God in the highest and on earth peace."

This means that shalom-making involves evangelism— bringing the good news to the people of our cities and nations so they may turn and receive Jesus as Savior and Lord and Friend. After declaring the good news that "God was in Christ" reconciling the world to Himself, the apostle Paul went on to say, "Therefore, we are ambassadors for Christ, as though God were making an appeal through us; we beg you on behalf of Christ, be reconciled to God" (2 Corinthians 5:20). "We beg

---

8 Vaclav Havel, "Forgetting We Are Not God," *First Things*, No. 51 (March 1995): 50. The original speech was given at Stanford University on September 29, 1994.

you, lay down your resistance to the Living God, and come home." Only the love of God in Jesus can melt resistant hearts. Peacemaking involves telling our contemporaries, in every way we can, of that love: declaring that it is safe to come out of hiding, that the Father against whom we have rebelled is waiting with outstretched arms (Luke 15). Shalom is a gift of God given to those who let God be God. That is the posture, the stance from which we make peace.

THE QUALIFICATIONS OF A PEACEMAKER

Second, I know the qualifications of a shalom-maker. They are the first six Beatitudes. In them the Prince of Peace is describing the people who have what it takes to be engaged in this Divine enterprise. And what a surprise!

1. Peacemakers are "poor in spirit." They recognize and admit their spiritual bankruptcy. They recognize and admit the lack of peace in their hearts. They recognize and admit the violence in their own hearts.

2. Peacemakers are "those who mourn." They grieve over the sinful condition of the world and their own hearts. They weep the tears of God Himself, who grieves over a humanity that turns its back.

3. Peacemakers are also "meek"—not weak, but gentle. They can resist temptation to take vengeance into their own hands, for they have thrown themselves on the King of kings and wait for Him to vindicate them.

4. Peacemakers also "hunger and thirst for righteousness." Their appetites have changed. They long to see God's right-relatedness be realized. They recognize that we live in one world, and they seek the good of the whole world, not just the good of their own empires. They treat other human beings with respect and not just as pawns in a grand chess game.

5. Peacemakers are "merciful." They do not need to give to others what others might rightly deserve; they give to others what they do not deserve: pardon and kindness. They are willing to put themselves in another person's, another culture's, and another nation's shoes.

6. And peacemakers are "pure in heart." They abhor deceit, hypocrisy, and manipulation. They can spot it in their own hearts and want it out. They want to see all of life in light of God's truth and grace. They recognize their own lust for power, their desire to control, and can distinguish it from the will of God. They simply seek the Face of Jesus.

According to the Prince of peace, it is "Beatitude People" who are agents of shalom. They are the ones who make peace in the world.

THE CONSEQUENCES OF PEACEMAKING

Third, I know what can happen to shalom-makers: they receive the approval and blessing of God. They sometimes receive the approval and blessing of people. And sometimes they receive other people's scorn and opposition.

If the first six Beatitudes describe the qualifications of peacemaking, the eighth Beatitude describes the consequence: "Blessed are those who are persecuted." Be engaged in the business of shalom-making and you just might encounter trouble. Jesus warns anyone who follows Him on the path of peacemaking that as rebellious human hearts resisted Him, they will resist them (see John 15:18-24). As E. Stanley Jones sadly observed, people "hate to be disturbed—even for the better."[9]

It would seem that no status quo can handle the poor in spirit and pure in heart, especially when the poor in spirit and pure in heart seek to let God be God, and they welcome His kingdom into the city. The status quo systems will have to pressure the disciples of Jesus into compromise or into silent acquiescence. If that does not work, the systems will seek to eliminate His disciples. Bishop Dom Helder Camara of Brazil said, "When I give food to the poor, they call me a saint. When I ask why the poor have no food, they call me a communist."[10] Shalom-makers often meet opposition and sometimes get hurt (which we will look at more in the next chapter).

THE COST OF PEACEMAKING

Fourth, I know that shalom-making involves sacrifice. That is, shalom-making involves a cross. How can it be otherwise? For how did God make peace with us?

---

9 Jones *The Christ of the Mount*, 77.
10 As given in the Introduction by Francis McDonagh to *Dom Helder Camara: Essential Writings* (Maryknoll, NY: Orbis Books, 2009), 11.

"For it was the Father's good pleasure for all the fullness to dwell in Christ, and through Him to reconcile all things to Himself, having made peace through the blood of His cross" (Colossians 1:19-20). "The chastening for our well-being [shalom] fell upon Him, and by His scourging we are healed" (Isaiah 53:5). The Living God makes shalom through sacrificial love, and so do we.

Thus, Jesus says to us later in the Sermon on the Mount, "I say to you, do not resist an evil person; but whoever slaps you on your right cheek, turn the other to him also" (Matthew 5:39). "Love your enemies and pray for those who persecute you" (Matthew 5:44). That is peacemaking, the way of the cross.

Paul exhorts the Christians in Rome: "Never pay back evil for evil to anyone.... But if your enemy is hungry, feed him, and if your enemy is thirsty, give him a drink.... Do not be overcome by evil, but overcome evil with good" (Romans 12:17, 20-21). That is peacemaking, the way of the cross.

So Dietrich Bonhoeffer concluded that the disciples of Jesus make peace "by choosing to endure suffering themselves rather than inflict it on others."[11]

Somewhere along the way, we have to come to terms with the fact that the cross is not only the source of our new life in Christ, but is also the pattern of our new life in Christ. The Prince of Peace who is our peace says to us, "If anyone wishes to come after Me, he must deny himself, and take up his cross daily and follow Me" (Luke 9:23). Shalom is made and experienced through the cross. Through the cross flows the blood that heals the wounds.

---

11 Bonhoeffer, *The Cost of Discipleship*, 126.

STEPS TO PEACEMAKING

I know one more thing about our vocation: It happens one step at a time. It happens by you and I making shalom in little ways in our little corners of our worlds. As the song goes, "Let there be peace on earth, and let it begin with me."[12] Or, as Paul exhorts believers: "If possible, so far as it depends on you, be at peace with all men [people]" (Romans 12:18).

Here are some little steps of peacemaking we might take today.

- We begin by affirming our identity and vocation in Jesus. We can say, "I am a peacemaker." By grace, we are children of God, sons and daughters of the Author of shalom, sisters and brothers of the Prince of peace. By grace, we have been granted the dignity of causality. "I am a partner in a Divine work."
- We can then acknowledge any resistance to God in our hearts. We can ask God to melt the resistance so we will let God be God.
- We can further acknowledge any anger in our hearts: anger against others, anger against self, and anger against God. We can ask God to heal the anger in our souls.
- We can further acknowledge any fear in our hearts. Fear holds us back from our great vocation. Acknowledge any fear, and ask Jesus to overcome it.

---

12 Jill Jackson Miller and Sy Miller, "Let There Be Peace on Earth," written in 1955.

- And then we can affirm the gospel again. We can say a fresh "amen" to God's *euangelion*. We can say with Jesus, "It is time. It is time for the kingdom of God to come near." Reaffirming the gospel revives perspective and courage and hope.

The kingdom has come and is coming. As Mortimer Arias of Bolivia put it, "Like a seed forcing its way upward through the soil, stones, and thistles of this world… like a fire that has been kindled over the earth; who can stop it?"[13] No one and nothing. No one and nothing can finally stand in the way of God's kingdom.

Shalom is coming—Easter morning guarantees that. Jesus' resurrection proclaims loud and clear that shalom will come. For the Prince of peace has defeated the greatest enemy of Peace; Jesus has defeated death. Shalom is coming.

Blessed, right-on, in sync are the shalom-makers, for they shall be called the children of God. What an incredible dignity!

---

13 Mortimer Arias, *Announcing the Reign of God: Evangelization and the Subversive Memory of Jesus* (Philadelphia: Fortress, 1984), 42.

9

BEATITUDE EIGHT
HAPPY SUBVERSIVES

MATTHEW 5:10

"Blessed are those who have been persecuted for the sake of righteousness, for theirs is the kingdom of heaven."

Blessed? The persecuted? Fortunate are those who are insulted? Congratulations? Right-on? "You lucky bums"?

Whenever I have preached the Beatitudes in a worship service, I have read the text, and then I have prayed something like this:

Lord Jesus, thank you for enabling Matthew the tax-collector to remember Your words and to write them down accurately for our sake. Will you now help us understand Your words? And more than understand, will you help us actually live into the reality Your words are describing?

When I come to this text, I'm not sure I want to pray that! Who wants to "live into the reality" of being persecuted? I gladly want Jesus to help me live into hungering and thirsting for righteousness, into purity of heart, into being merciful, into being a peacemaker. But into being persecuted?

Helmut Thielicke, a great theologian-preacher of the twentieth century, writes of the eighth Beatitude:

> What a ghastly prospect! It makes one ask in all seriousness how Jesus could ever have gained disciples with an appeal like that. And then does it not sound like sheer mockery for him to go on and say, in the face of the tortures of body and soul to which they were actually exposed, "Rejoice and be glad!" If that is not mockery (and surely it cannot be that) then there must be some great mystery here which we do not see.[1]

PRELIMINARY OBSERVATIONS

Before we wrestle with the eighth Beatitude, let us make a number of exegetical observations.

First, this is a "double" beatitude. For some reason, Jesus repeats and re-states this one. Is it because it is the one He knows we would rather not hear? Or is it because this is the one Jesus Himself felt the most?

Second, in repeating the Beatitude, Jesus shifts the pronouns. He moves from the third person "they" to the second person "you." No longer is the subject a theoretical "they"; the

---

1 Thielicke, *Life Can Begin Again*, 13.

subject is now "you"…"you men and women who sit before Me on the mountaintop." And you, reading this book. And me.

Third, for the first time Jesus brings Himself into the picture: "On account of Me." He has, of course, been there in the other seven beatitudes, as we have seen. But in the eighth, He makes it explicit: "On account of Me." It is as though Jesus is saying, "I am the problem: you will find yourselves in a difficult place because of Me."

And fourth, note carefully the reason for the persecution. Jesus is not blessing those who get persecuted for being obnoxious in peacemaking, or those who get persecuted for being tactless, or who are culturally insensitive as they bear witness in the world. Jesus is not congratulating those who are persecuted for being dogmatically dogmatic or narrow-mindedly narrow-minded. Jesus is not applauding the thrill-seeking confrontationist, or those with a "victim complex." Jesus is blessing those who find themselves in trouble "because of righteousness" and "because of Me." "For the sake of right-relatedness" and "on account of Me."

"Right-relatedness" and Jesus go together. For right-relatedness is most clearly manifest in Jesus; Jesus is righteousness personified. This is why the "hunger and thirst for righteousness" He blesses in the fourth Beatitude turns out to be a hunger and thirst for Him. It is why the hunger and thirst for Him always issues in a hunger and thirst for right-relatedness. Jesus is blessing those who experience opposition and reproach because of their craving to see relationships work and because of their relationship with Him. Rejoice! And be exceedingly glad! According to Luke, Jesus adds "and leap for joy!" Really?

WHY BEING PERSECUTED IS TO BE CONGRATULATED

Throughout this book, I have been emphasizing that the qualities Jesus blesses are not natural human qualities. We do not produce them. They are the product of Jesus' gospel. He comes into our lives with His evangel, His good news—His news of the nearness and in-breaking of the kingdom of God. And when He and His news get hold of us, we become poor in spirit, we begin to mourn, we become meek/gentle, we hunger and thirst in a new way, we become pure in heart, we begin to make peace… and we get persecuted. Oh, He also uses us to win others to Himself! But sometimes, we get persecuted.

So, I want to ask "why?" Why is being persecuted a mark of being evangelized by Jesus?

This is not a theoretical matter. Believers all over the world are experiencing persecution today, some in really painful ways. According to David Barrett, editor of the *World Christian Encyclopedia*, if we total up the number of Christians martyred for their faith in the twentieth century, it works out to an average of 454,000 a year.[2] It is estimated that over 200 million Christians in 60 countries are currently being denied basic

---

2 David B. Barrett and Todd M. Johnson, *World Christian Trends AD 30–AD 2200: Interpreting the Annual Christian Megacensus* (Pasadena, CA: William Carey Library, 2001), 229.

human rights because of their allegiance to Jesus.[3]

In Luke's Gospel, Jesus adds the line: "Woe to you when all men speak well of you, for their fathers used to treat the false prophets in the same way" (Luke 6:26). Sobering.

So, why is being persecuted a mark of those who have turned around and embraced Jesus and His gospel?

For one basic reason: the reason Jesus gave that night before handing Himself over to death, when He gathered the first band of disciples together around a table in an Upper Room somewhere in downtown Jerusalem. "If the world hates you, you know that it has hated Me before it hated you.... Remember the word that I said to you, 'A slave is not greater than his master.' If they persecuted Me, they will persecute you" (John 15:18, 20).

It is as simple as that. If the old order of things, human society organizing itself without God (the meaning of the term "world"), cannot handle the Master, it will not be able to handle the Master's servants. If the old order of things cannot tolerate the Righteous One, it will not be able to tolerate those who seek to follow Him and reflect His righteousness. The rest of the New Testament tells us that persecution, of one sort or another, is inevitable for the followers of the Persecuted One. The apostle Paul had to encourage his colleague Timothy—

---

3 World Evangelical Alliance, "Geneva Report 2005: A Perspective on Global Religious Freedom: Challenges Facing Christian Communities," available at http://www.worldevangelicals.org/ resources/view.htm?id=116 (accessed 4 March 2013).

who tended to be a bit timid—"indeed, all who desire to live godly in Christ Jesus will be persecuted" (2 Timothy 3:12).

The question therefore becomes, "Why was Jesus persecuted?" "How lovely on the mountains," says the prophet Isaiah, "are the feet of Him who brings good news"—the good news of God's shalom (Isaiah 52:7). Why would anyone want to insult or hurt a Man who brings good news, who brings shalom? Why would anyone want to get rid of a Man who heals the sick, who sets free those possessed by evil, who forgives sinners and welcomes the imperfect into His family?

Clearly, Jesus was not persecuted for being obnoxious, or for being tactless or insensitive in the way He lived and spoke His good news. He was not running around shoving His gospel down people's throats. He did at one point issue a series of "woes" against the entrenched leadership of the religious establishment ("Woe to you hypocrites…" Matthew 23), but that was long after the establishment had hardened its heart against Him, long after they had resolved to eliminate Him. Why was Jesus—the most beautiful human being who ever lived—persecuted?

As I see it, for three reasons: He experienced opposition and scorn simply by being, doing, and speaking. Jesus experienced insult and harm by being righteous, by doing righteousness, and by speaking righteously.

PERSECUTION FOR BEING RIGHTEOUS

First, Jesus got into trouble by simply being righteous. Righteousness, especially perfect righteousness, is experienced by us unrighteous either as a blessing or as a threat. It all depends on whether we are willing to acknowledge our unrighteousness and want help to be righteous. Because we do not on our own like to face our own unrighteousness, righteousness—especially perfect righteousness—is usually experienced as a threat. Oh, at first it is welcomed, even celebrated... but not for long. The mere presence of righteousness, justice, and goodness calls for change. Righteousness need not say a word. It need only enter the room and be there. Without speaking a word, the presence of righteousness exposes the rottenness. And we either open up to the goodness or we will feel we need to get rid of it.

Jesus of Nazareth is Goodness incarnate. He is light, and in Him there is no darkness at all. His mere being in a place exposes attitudes and actions of darkness, and we either open up to the light, turn around and let the light heal us, or we seek to get rid of the light. If the world (human society organizing itself without God) hated Goodness Himself, what will the world do with those who seek and reflect His goodness? When He imparts His righteousness to us, we begin to change; we are not made perfect, but we do begin to change. We slowly but surely become non-conformists. As Flannery O'Connor is reputed to have said: "You shall know the truth and the truth shall make you odd."[4]

Hagios is the Biblical term: saints, holy ones. Not in the sense of being perfect, but in the sense of being set-apart, other-than, different-from, marching to the beat of a different drummer. Jesus is different, wonderfully different! He is not *of*

---

4 Ralph C. Wood, *Flannery O'Connor and the Christ-Haunted South* (Grand Rapids: William B. Eerdmans, 2004), 160.

the world—*in* it, all the way, but not *of* it in any way. His mere Presence, His radiant Goodness, can therefore be experienced as a threat. That is the first reason He was persecuted—simply for being righteous.

PERSECUTION FOR DOING RIGHTEOUSNESS

Second, Jesus got in trouble by simply doing righteousness. He was not merely present; He acted in ways that rocked the boat. Rocked the boat is putting it mildly! He disturbed the status quo. More to the point, He subverted the status quo. Not that Jesus went around as some kind of rabble-rouser. In fact, He shied away from public events and public attractions. He simply went around living His gospel, doing right-relatedness. Doing righteousness in an unrighteous world always rocks the boat. Jesus' announcement of the nearness of the kingdom of God and Jesus' full embodiment of the different values of the kingdom automatically challenged everything out of sync with the kingdom. His doing righteousness set up a clashing of kingdoms, or "kingdoms in conflict," as Charles Colson put it.[5] Mortimer Arias put it this way: "The coming of the kingdom means a permanent confrontation of worlds. The kingdom is a question mark in the midst of the established ideas and answers developed by people and societies."[6]

Jesus began to disturb things by always bringing the "wrong people" to the party. "This man receives sinners and eats with them" was the charge leveled against Him (Luke

---

5 Charles Colson with Ellen Santilli Vaughn, *Kingdoms in Conflict* (Grand Rapids: Zondervan, 1987).
6 Arias, *Announcing the Reign of God*, 46-47.

15:2), and it was said in great disgust. Jesus' way with people upset the religious establishment's whole concept of righteousness. They taught that people had to shape up before being allowed to "come home" to the Father. Jesus taught that all people had to do was "come home"; the shaping up would come later. The religious establishment could not handle Jesus' revelation of God's righteousness. That is, they could not handle grace. Jacques Ellul once said, "Grace is odious to us."[7] Grace says, "You are not making it on your own." Grace says, "You will never make it on your own." Grace says, "You need Me." Grace therefore subverts our pride, our desire to be able to sing, "I did it my way."

Jesus disturbed things in another way: He violated many of the human rules made to supposedly bring about righteousness. For example, Jesus knowingly violated many of the Sabbath rules. He did not violate the Sabbath; He did not violate God's good commandment. He simply questioned and subverted many of the human-made rules and regulations that had developed around God's commandment. Why? Because the human rules and regulations were unrighteous! They had nothing to do with right-relatedness, especially right-relatedness with God. The rules oppressed people's spirits and drove them farther away from His Father's heart. Jesus of Nazareth was crucified because of the way He acted on the Sabbath.

Jesus rocked the boat in yet another way: He caused the kingdom to be manifested. He actually did "kingdom stuff." For example, Jesus encounters a man near the Sea of

---

7 Jacques Ellul, *The Subversion of Christianity* (Grand Rapids: Wm. B. Eerdmans, 1986), 159.

Galilee who had been demonized, held captive by a legion of evil spirits. Jesus orders the spirits to release the man. The spirits beg Jesus to let them go into a herd of pigs. Jesus grants the request, and the herd rushes down a steep bank into the sea. Mark tells us that "about two thousand of them" were drowned (Mark 5:13). The people of the town rejoiced, right? A human being had been set free and they rejoiced, right? No, sadly. They were angry and begged Jesus to leave their town. Why? Because simply by doing righteousness, Jesus was upsetting their value system.

If the world systems—secular or religious—could not handle Jesus doing His gospel, what will they do with His disciples doing His gospel?

Look at what happened to the apostle Paul. He did not set out to disturb the status quo. All he did was set out to announce Jesus' good news. I repeat: Paul did not set out to subvert anything. All he set out to do was announce Jesus' gospel. In the city of Ephesus, a city of about 225,000 people at the time, Paul found himself in the middle of a riot and had to leave the city (Acts 19). Why? Because he tried to start a riot? Not at all. All he did was announce the gospel, and people responded. They turned around, embraced Jesus as Savior, and began to follow Him as Master. Why then the riot? Well, many of the Ephesians practiced magical arts. As an expression of their new life in Jesus, they came together and burned all their occult books. Also, many of the Ephesians had been ardent devotees of the goddess Artemis, or Diana. Before coming to Jesus they used to buy statues of Diana. After coming to Jesus they no longer needed the statues. The Ephesian economy was built around the worship of Diana. The silversmiths who made the statues were losing money. So a certain Demetrius incited other merchants into a riot against Paul. All Paul did was righteousness. All Paul did was announce the good news, which brought people into right-relatedness with God. He did not intend to disturb the status quo. It just happened, as it always does. The gospel always messes with idols. And therefore, slowly but surely, it messes with a way of life built on idols.

I had the privilege of serving as the pastor of Union Church in Manila from 1985 to 1989. When we arrived in the Philippines in the fall of 1985, things were very tense. People who spoke out against the dictatorial ways of Ferdinand Marcos were disappearing; some of their bodies turned up floating in the river that goes through the city. We could feel the tension everywhere. Soon after I began preaching at Union Church, a group of pastors and priests had a welcome lunch for me. They reminded me that I would never know who was in the sanctuary on any given Sunday, so I needed to be very careful with what I said. Their advice to me was "just preach the gospel." Good advice! But the implication was "and you will then be safe in Manila." Be safe? "Just stick to preaching the gospel," and you will be safe? What gospel are you referring to? Not Jesus' gospel. Jesus' gospel is, "The kingdom of God is invading the city." How can you "just stick to preaching the gospel" and think you will be safe? As long as we keep the "kingdom stuff" in the private, personal realm, we can avoid conflict. As long as we silently acquiesce to the idols of our time, we can avoid getting caught in the crunch as kingdoms collide. But once we let the kingdom "out of the bag," so to speak, things begin to happen. Jesus was persecuted because he was doing his gospel of the kingdom. He was turning things upside down so that they could be right-side up.

PERSECUTION FOR SPEAKING RIGHTEOUSNESS

Third, Jesus got in trouble by simply speaking righteousness about Himself. For example, He would walk up to people—like fishermen and tax-collectors—and say, "Follow Me." That is not an invitation—"Say, would you like to follow Me?" It is a command—"Here, behind Me." Who is this guy who thinks He can just walk into anyone's life and order a change of agenda?

And there are those claims He makes about Himself, especially the "I AM" claims. "I am the Light of the world; he who follows Me will not walk in the darkness, but will have the Light of life" (John 8:12). "I am the Door," enter by Me (John 10:9). "I am the vine... apart from Me you can do nothing" (John 15:5). "I am the resurrection and the life; he who believes in Me will live even if he dies" (John 11:25). He says those loaded words matter-of-factly; there's no fanfare, no hype. He just says them.

"I am the Bread of Life. You need Me more than you need your next meal" (see John 6:35). Whoa dude!

"I am the way, and the truth, and the life" (John 14:6). Jesus does not say *a* way, *a* truth, *a* life—He says "I am *the* Way, *the* Truth, and *the* Life." "Jesus, if you would just say 'a' you would not get Yourself in trouble." To which He answers, "What am I supposed to do, deny Who I am?" "Who are You, Jesus?" the authorities ask in white-hot anger. "Before Abraham was, I Am," He replies. And John tells us they took up stones to throw at Jesus (John 8:58-59).

The way Jesus speaks about Himself subverts our fundamental presuppositions about God, about ourselves, and about life itself. Sometimes it is too much to handle. If some people cannot handle Jesus speaking about Himself so outrageously, what are they to do with those who repeat His outrageous claims?

And what will they do with those who seek to live out the implications of His claims?

Peter and John were going to the temple one day to pray. On the steps lay a crippled man, begging. He put out his hand hoping for money. Peter said, "I do not possess silver and gold, but what I do have I give to you: In the name of Jesus Christ the Nazarene—walk!" (Acts 3:6). And the man did. And the city rejoiced, right? Some did. But the religious authorities did not. They hauled Peter and John in for interrogation, asking, "By what power, or in what name, have you done this?" (Acts 4:7). Peter responded, "By the name of Jesus Christ the Nazarene" (Acts 4:10). Now, if Peter had just left it at that he might have been set free. But he did not leave it at that, for he could not leave it at that. So he went on to say, "And there is salvation in no one else; for there is no other name under heaven that has been given among men by which we must be saved" (Acts 4:12).

No other name. That is what got him in trouble: what the theologians call "the scandal of particularity"—the claim that life is found in Jesus and only in Jesus. You may have personally experienced what Peter and John faced. Just say, "Jesus is one of many healers," or "Jesus is one of many lords," and we are welcomed at the Feast of Pluralism in our age of tolerance. But say what Peter said—that is, muster up the courage and echo the way Jesus spoke of Himself, and say, "There is no other healer but Jesus," or "There is no other lord but Jesus"—and we will be asked to leave the feast, or worse.

We will be accused of being intolerant. But the fact is, it has nothing to do with intolerance. It has everything to do with *righteousness*. It has everything to do with faithfulness to a relationship with Jesus. He made the claims; we didn't. What are we supposed to do? Water them down? Give in to the spirit of the age, and deny who He is? We cannot. We can be kind and respectful, meek and gentle. But we cannot be unfaithful to who He claims to be.

Blessed? Right-on? Congratulations? To those who are persecuted for the sake of righteousness? Yes!

In sync are you when people insult you, and persecute you, and say all kinds of evil against you falsely on account of Me. Rejoice! And be glad! Rejoice and be glad? I know how I feel when I'm only mildly criticized. I know how I feel when I'm only snickered at because of what I say about Jesus. Rejoice and be glad?

Why, Lord? Because "you have a great reward in heaven." OK. And because you are not alone, you join a long line of others, "for so they persecuted the prophets who were before you." OK, that helps. And because "yours is the kingdom." Not, "yours will be the kingdom," but "yours is the kingdom." Is—now.

Jesus is putting everything in perspective. It is because God's glorious kingdom is already breaking into one's life that he or she is treated the way Jesus was treated. It is because Jesus' gospel is already taking hold that we are getting caught in the crunch. With that perspective, I just might be able to keep my cool. And I may even be able to bless the persecutor.

Mortimer Arias sums it up for me:

the arrival of the kingdom produces a crisis.... It is like a sword that draws a dividing line and cuts through the most intimate and sacred relationships and loyalties, and subordinates any former value or commitment.... The kingdom is reversal and, as such, the permanent subverter of human orders. The proclaimer of this kingdom could not expect any other treatment than the one reserved for the subversives in human history.[8]

---

8 Arias, *Announcing the Reign of God*, 42–43.

10

CONCLUSION

At the beginning of our study in Jesus' Beatitudes, I invited you—so to speak—to take a seat with me at the feet of Jesus, and to listen to Him. I suggested that we sit before Jesus as He painted a portrait of people whom He is drawing to Himself and in whom He is causing His kingdom to invade and occupy. Having listened to and grappled with His revolutionary words, what should we now do? We must do something, right? Like those who were sitting in that natural amphitheater along the Sea of Galilee, we too have to do something with what we have heard, right?

So, in this conclusion, I invite you to join me and kneel before Jesus. I invite you to do the most important thing we must do—pray. This is what I am driven to each time I spend time in the Beatitudes: to pray, asking the living Jesus to make it all real in my life, in your life, in the life of the church, and in the life of the world.

Lord Jesus:

It is with joy that we confess you as Savior and Lord. Indeed, there is no other Savior and Lord but You.

We thank You for speaking Your Beatitudes, for speaking the Divine Blessing upon us. We are humbled that You love us enough to give us Your perspective on what it means to be human in our world. We are deeply humbled that You love us enough to speak Your kingdom into our world!

We acknowledge that we are indeed poor in spirit. May this always be our posture before You, so that You are free do in us what only You can do.

We do mourn over the state of our world, especially in its rejection of You. And we grieve that we are not all that You long for us to be. We are moved by the realization that You mourn with us, and that Your mourning will soon turn into joy, and thus, ours too.

We affirm that gentleness is the way You want us to be in all our relationships. In You we see that the gentle do in fact inherit the goodness of creation. Make us like You!

Oh how we hunger and thirst for You to put all things right. We give You thanks for all the ways You are doing this right now, but we long for that Day when Your great craving will be fulfilled in a fully righteous world.

How can we ever adequately thank You for Your mercy? You are Mercy. Holy Mercy. Help us to so drink of Your mercy that we have the strength to extend mercy to all we encounter. Help us hear in the brokenness around us the cry, "Someone have mercy on me!"

You know that we want to be pure in heart. We confess that we cannot make this happen in our lives.

Only You, the Pure One, can work such a miracle in our souls. Please, dear Friend of Sinners, make it so. You know how much we want to see: to see You, to see the Father. We know that one Day we will. But grant that every day before that Day we can see what is see-able right now!

Makers of shalom? Oh what dignity You bestow on us! Free us from all that gets in the way of cooperating with You in Your great work in the world; equip us with all the grace we need to be people of peace. We want to be known as the children of the Peace-Making God in all the places we live and work.

And Jesus, we know that as we seek to live in sync with You and Your agenda in this age, we could find ourselves in trouble. We would rather it not happen, but we do thank You for warning us, and making it clear why it happens. Should we be persecuted on account of You, please so work in us that we can be like Stephen, who when he was being unjustly stoned, followed Your lead and prayed, "Father, forgive them; they do not know what they are doing."

There simply is no one like You!

To You be all the glory, as, with the Father and the Holy Spirit, You reign now and forevermore.

Amen.

QUESTIONS FOR

SMALL GROUP STUDIES

Jesus first spoke the Beatitudes to a group of people. This suggests that we can best understand and live His words in community. The following questions were prepared by my colleague in ministry, Doug Hills. Having worked through the book and knowing the kinds of questions I have posed in other contexts, Doug came up with this helpful tool for group interaction.

INTRODUCTION: THE EMERGING OF A NEW HUMANITY

1. What is the most impressive speech you ever heard?
2. How do you feel when you hear the Beatitudes? Do you ever act as if they are either "frustrating idealism or oppressive legalism"?
3. If you were asked to define the gospel in one sentence, what would you say?
4. What would it look like for you to repent and believe in the good news described in this chapter?
5. Suggestions for prayer:
   a. The chapter starts with the invitation to give Jesus a fresh hearing. Pray that as you study, you would hear these familiar words in a fresh way.

b. Ask that you would be able to go beyond just reading these words, and move deeper into the reality
that Jesus is describing in these Beatitudes.

CHAPTER 1: PRELIMINARY OBSERVATIONS

1. What word or phrase would you suggest to translate
makarios ("blessed") in today's culture?

2. Which of the preliminary observations mentioned in
this chapter surprised you?

3. Which of these preliminary observations will change
how you read the Beatitudes? How will you read them
differently?

4. Suggestions for prayer:

a. The chapter ends by reminding us of the supernatu-
ral character of the Beatitudes. Thank God for
this fact!

b. Pray that God would continue to infuse His grace,
and change you into more of who He wants you
to be.

c. Spend some time before Him, seeing if there are
areas of your life in which you need to more
deeply embrace Him and His reign.

CHAPTER 2: BEATITUDE ONE: OH, YOU FORTUNATE PAUPERS!

1. What do you think of when you think of poverty?
What pictures come to mind when you hear of
"the poor"?

2. Darrell says that the gospel is the announcement that the "future is spilling over into the present." What does that mean? Describe some places where you see this happening.

3. Read the parable of the Pharisee and the tax-collector (Luke 18:9-14). If someone listened to you prayers this week, which of the two characters do you think they would say you are more like?

4. How does this Beatitude give you hope as you read the rest of the Sermon on the Mount (and the rest of the New Testament)?

5. Suggestions for prayer:

   a. One prayer that has been prayed through church history is known as the "Jesus Prayer": "Lord Jesus Christ, Son of God, have mercy on me, the sinner." Say this prayer slowly, followed by 10-15 seconds of silence. Do this several times, reflecting on the words.

   b. As you acknowledge your spiritual poverty, rejoice that God is the kingdom-giver, who "gives generously to all without finding fault" (James 1:5). Thank Him for the good gifts that He delights to give us.

CHAPTER 3: BEATITUDE TWO: GOD'S ACHING VISIONARIES

1. What is the first experience of grief and mourning that you remember? How was the grief expressed (or not expressed)?

2. Can you relate a time when your sadness was a launching pad to growth?

3. This chapter describes several times when Jesus cried. How surprising was it to think of Jesus breaking out in "uncontrollable weeping"? How comfortable are you with this idea?

4. As you look around the world today, what specifically causes you to say, "This is not how it should be"?

5. Suggestions for prayer:

    a. Spend some time asking for a tender heart—in light of the reality of our sins, the needs of others, and the way things are in the world.

    b. Pray for those who you know are mourning at this time—that they would know the comfort that comes from the "Father of Compassion and the God of all comfort" (2 Corinthians 1:3).

CHAPTER 4: BEATITUDE THREE: THE INVINCIBLE

1. Before you read this chapter, how would you have explained "meekness"? How is your understanding different after reading the chapter?

2. Describe someone you know who embodies meekness. Looking at the characteristics of the meek in Psalm 37, which ones are most difficult for you?

3. What does it mean to you that the meek will inherit the earth?

4. Suggestions for prayer:

    a. The meek "roll their lives, their cares, their reputations onto the Lord" (Stuart Briscoe). Take time to list the things that you are concerned about, and then give them to God to "let the Lord worry about it all."

b. "To belong to Jesus Christ is to be granted the privilege of living in the palace with him, playing with His toys, and enjoying His backyard." Thank God for the beauty of the earth and the fact that He gives it to His own.

CHAPTER 5: BEATITUDE FOUR: ALIVE IN A GOD-SIZED CRAVING

1. What is the most hungry you have ever been?
2. The chapter tells us that righteousness is all about relationship. How does this change the way you think of righteousness?
3. Four basic relationships were described in this chapter—with the earth, with others, with the self, and with God. Is there one of these with which it is harder for you to maintain a good relationship?
4. What does it look like for us to be thirsting for righteousness? What are the marks that we are growing in our hungering for right-relatedness?
5. Suggestions for prayer:
   a. Sit in silence for a minute and let God speak to you about any part of your relationships (with the earth, with others, with the self, and with Him) that needs to be healed. Ask Him to show you if there is anything you can do to help heal the relationship.

b. Pray through Psalm 63, a prayer David wrote in the desert of Judah.

CHAPTER 6: BEATITUDE FIVE: MERCY!

1. Describe a time when you deserved something bad (punishment, a speeding ticket, etc.), and were given mercy. How did it make you feel?

2. Read through the parable of the Good Samaritan (Luke 10:25-37), and look at how he extended mercy to the man in need. What were some of the reasons the priest and the Levite may have chosen not to extend mercy?

3. Can you think of someone specific to whom you should be extending mercy? What would that look like?

4. Darrell ends the chapter by looking at whether only those who show mercy receive mercy. How does he answer this question? Does his answer satisfy you?

5. Suggestions for prayer:
   a. Reflect on the great mercy that God has shown to you, and thank him for how He has not given you what you've deserved, but has shown kindness to you in your need and pardoned your debts.
   b. Pray through the Lord's Prayer (Matthew 6:9-13). Finish by reading verses 14 and 15 out loud.

CHAPTER 7: BEATITUDE SIX: SEE GOD? REALLY?

1. What is the most beautiful or awe-inspiring thing you have ever seen? Describe it for the others in the group.

2. What do you think Jesus means when he promises that we shall see God?

3. What does it mean to be pure in heart? What would that look like in your daily life?

4. The chapter finishes with a dialogue between Saint Francis and Brother Leo. What was Francis trying to help Leo see? Which point of view do you find yourself identifying more with?

5. Suggestions for prayer:
   a. Pray slowly through Psalm 139.
   b. Spend some time describing what you have seen in Jesus of Nazareth, and thanking Him for showing you more of who God is.

CHAPTER 8: BEATITUDE SEVEN: SHALOM-MAKERS

1. Who do you think of when you think of a peacemaker? Describe her or him.

2. How does each of the other Beatitudes round out the portrait of those who are peacemakers?

3. What can we expect as we follow Jesus into making shalom?

4. What does it mean to be called "children of God"?

5. Suggestions for prayer:
   a. In silence, allow God to point out any areas in your life that lack the shalom of God, and then pray for these situations.
   b. Pray the "Prayer of Saint Francis":
      Lord, make me an instrument of your peace,

Where there is hatred, let me sow love;

Where there is injury, pardon;

Where there is doubt, faith;

Where there is despair, hope;

Where there is darkness, light;

Where there is sadness, joy.

O Divine Master,

grant that I may not so much seek to be

consoled, as to console;

to be understood, as to understand;

to be loved, as to love.

For it is in giving that we receive.

It is in pardoning that we are pardoned,

and it is in dying that we are born to

Eternal Life.

Amen.

CHAPTER 9: BEATITUDE EIGHT: HAPPY SUBVERSIVES

1. Describe a time when being, doing, or speaking righteousness cost you something.

2. Can you think of other examples (from the Bible or from history) where people have been persecuted for being, doing, or speaking righteousness?

3. The chapter discusses the "scandal of particularity"— the exclusive claim that Jesus is the only way. How comfortable are you with making this claim? How tolerant is our society of such a claim?

4. What is promised in this Beatitude for those who are persecuted?

5. Suggestions for prayer:

   a. As the chapter points out, many Christians today face severe persecution. Research a place of persecution and pray for the believers there.

   b. As we finish this study of the Beatitudes, pray through them one at a time, asking that God would continue His work in making you more like Jesus, and making these Beatitudes more and more true of you.

FOR FURTHER READING

The footnotes throughout the book will show you some of the many resources that I have used in my study of the Beatitudes. For further reading, I especially commend:

Barclay, William. *The Beatitudes and the Lord's Prayer for Everyman*. New York: Harper & Row, 1963.

Bonhoeffer, Dietrich. *The Cost of Discipleship*. Revised Edition. New York: MacMillan Publishing, 1959.

Boice, James M. *The Sermon on the Mount: An Exposition*. Grand Rapids: Zondervan, 1972.

Bruner, F. Dale. *The Christbook: A Historical/Theological Commentary (Matthew 1-12)*. Waco, TX: Word Books, 1987.

Guelich, Robert. *The Sermon on the Mount: A Foundation for Understanding*. Dallas: Word Publishing, 1982.

Gundry, Robert H. *Matthew: A Commentary on His Handbook for a Mixed Church under Persecution*. Grand Rapids: Wm. B. Eerdmans, 1995.

Jones, E. Stanley. *The Christ of the Mount: A Working Philosophy of Life*. Nashville: Abingdon, 1931.

Lapide, Pinchas. *The Sermon on the Mount: Utopia or Program for Action?* Maryknoll, NY: Orbis Books, 1986.

Lloyd-Jones, D. Martyn. *Studies in the Sermon on the Mount, Volume 1.* Grand Rapids: Eerdmans, 1959.

Stott, John R.W. *Christian Counter-Culture: The Message of the Sermon on the Mount.* Downers Grove: InterVarsity Press, 1978.

Talbert, Charles H. *Reading the Sermon on the Mount: Character Formation and Decision Making in Matthew 5-7.* Grand Rapids: Baker Academic, 2006.

Thielicke, Helmut. *Life Can Begin Again: Sermons on the Sermon on the Mount.* Philadelphia: Fortress, 1963.

CPSIA information can be obtained at www.ICGtesting.com
Printed in the USA
LVOW11s0415230615

443433LV00002B/142/P